Daughter, Where's Your Crown?

Daughter, Where's Your Crown?

EXAMINE BIBLICAL VIRTUE IN THE
LIFE OF RUTH AND PROVERBS 31

Kathy Farley

CrossLink Publishing

CrossLink Publishing
558 E. Castle Pines Pkwy, Ste B4117
Castle Rock, CO 80108
www.crosslinkpublishing.com

Ordering Information:
Quantity sales. Special discounts are available on quantity purchases by corporations, associations, and others. For details, contact the "Special Sales Department" at the address above.

Daughter, Where's Your Crown?/Farley —1st ed.

ISBN 978-1-63357-121-1

Library of Congress Control Number: 2017955608

First edition: 10 9 8 7 6 5 4 3 2 1

In Loving Memory of

Beata Baker

1972 – 2012

Only God knew how desperately I needed the friendship of this precious woman. He brought her to Murray, Kentucky, all the way from Wisla, Poland, in August 2008. We connected soon after when she began coming to a Sunday night Bible study I was teaching on the names of God. Our love for God and His Word (and Reese's Peanut Butter Cups) bonded us together as sisters and special friends. What a rare and perfect gift, one that I am so grateful for!

**Dedicated to my beautiful daughters,
Nicole and Tiffany**

*You are both Proverbs 31 women. You are an inspiration to me as
you love your God first, then your husbands, children, and others
God has entrusted to you. I am so proud of the women you are
and who you will become as your submissive journey with God
continues. May you always know how special you are to the One
who made you and empowers you to live a life pleasing to Him.*

I love you,

Mom

Contents

Introduction

Dear God,

I thank You for what You have taught me through this study. My desire is to be more like Jesus. I believe that the one reading these words has that same desire or she wouldn't be looking at this study.

Lord, may all of us called by Your name and saved by Your grace through faith in Christ Jesus be prepared by Your Word and equipped by Your Spirit. Lord, may our lives be free of bondage that hinders us from walking in Your fullness. May our only chains be that which connects us to You.

Creator, I ask You to touch the mind and heart of the one who is praying this prayer with me. Create in her a will and desire for change.

Savior, I ask You to assure her of the love that You have for her. The sacrifice You made on her behalf was not only for eternal security but also for her security now as she lives on this earth. Lord, reveal to her in the pages to come that freedom in You will only come through obedience to Your Word and dependence upon Your Spirit.

Sustainer, allow the one reading these words to feel Your power in her and over her. We were not meant to live life alone. It is by You, Lord, that we live at all. Open our mind's eye to see You as the Israelites did in the cloud by day and the fire by night. You and only You will hold us up as we persevere in this adventurous journey called life.

Jesus, finally I ask You to use the lessons herein to demonstrate Your conviction, encouragement, and grace over every stronghold in the reader's life.

Master, may the words turn her heart and may she surrender everything that is holding her back from the life of freedom in You.

Thank You, Lord, that it is Your desire that we give defeat back to Satan, the Deceiver, and that we take what belongs to us, a purposed life wrapped in Love. May each one of us realize the precious gift of life you have given us. Help us hold Your promises ever so close to our grateful hearts. In the precious name of Jesus, I pray.

Amen.

Before we begin:

Recently, I told my friend and mentor, Virginia, that I was writing a Bible study on the Proverbs 31 woman. She jokingly said, "You mean that super woman who can do everything perfectly, the one who stays up late and gets up early. That woman?"

I laughed and said, "Well, yes ... but... "

She interrupted me and added, "I tore that page out of my Bible!"

Of course, I knew she was kidding and we both laughed.

As I shared with Virginia that day some of what God was teaching me through research and listening for His guidance through His Word, she raised some questions (just like a good mentor) that caused me to want more. I began to dig a little deeper. What I realized was that King Lemuel's mother was deeply committed to the Lord. Out of her faith, she boldly directed her son in the Lord's direction. Her conviction to the ways of the Lord not only extended to her son but also to the wife he would choose, which would impact her grandchildren and the generations to come.

Verses 1 through 9 are so important, and for too long we have skipped over them. Without the foundation set through these verses, we can easily become overwhelmed by this biblical superwoman.

My heart's desire from the beginning, when this project was only a thought in my mind, was to write a study for busy women who want to go deeper with the limited time they have to give. What you will find as you begin this study is that it's divided into two parts.

Part 1 consists of the first 9 lessons on Proverbs 31:1–9. They are longer in length, and, therefore, require more time each day. Hang in there and go slowly. If you can only get through half of a lesson each day, that's okay. I do recommend that if you divide the lessons up, when you come back to complete the lesson, read through the portion you have completed as a refresher before continuing on.

Part 2 (Proverbs 31:10-31) begins with a review of Part 1. The lessons in Part 2 will go quicker because the foundation has already been laid. The layout of the lessons has a different look than Part 1. Don't get hung up on that—just be faithful in doing the work.

There are four "Royal Reflections" within Part 2. I hope these will be "Selah" time-outs for you, time to pause and breathe in who you are in God's family.

My prayer is that the Lord will clear up a few misconceptions about the Proverbs 31 woman. But most importantly, that each one who goes through this study will be drawn to Him as He teaches the lessons He wants to personally give.

This study has given me fresh insights and, as always, I have experienced God as all-powerful and all-loving through the pages of His Word.

So, if you're ready, let's begin *Daughter, Where's Your Crown?* Oh, by the way, the title of this study will become clear to you as we walk through this time each day with God. I am honored to study with you.

Kathy

Part 1

ADVICE FROM THE KING'S MOTHER

TO HER SON ON HOW

A WISE KING SHOULD REIGN

Out of a Momma's Mouth

PROVERBS 31:1

Chapter 31 of the Book of Proverbs is presented as advice that Lemuel's mother gave to him first about how a wise king should reign. Then starting with verse 10, she detailed the attributes of the kind of wife he should desire.

KJV	NASB	NIV
The words of King Lemuel, the prophecy that his mother taught him.	The words of King Lemuel, the oracle which his mother taught him.	The sayings of King Lemuel—an oracle his mother taught him.

I was thinking today about all the advice I have given over the years. Some of it I would love to stuff back in my mouth never to have spoken at all. Now looking back, I see that at times, the advice I gave was so worldly. Oh how I wish those words had been words directing someone to Jesus.

Let's break down each part of the verse:

The words (sayings) from the Hebrew *dabar* signifies a spoken word or speech: advice.[1]

of King Lemuel

Bible scholars differ on the identity of this king (pronounced Lem-yoo-uhl). Many of the early Jewish rabbis identified him with Solomon (the names Lemuel and Solomon have the same Hebrew meaning). Here in Proverbs 31 is the only mention of him (vv. 1 and 4). I was hoping my research would lead me directly to this king. I was disappointed at first to see the different opinions on his identity until the meaning of his name leaped off the page at me. His name means "for God" or "belonging to God." Whoever this man was, he belonged to God!

prophecy (oracle) that his mother taught him.

Normally the word prophecy brings to mind a prophet from the Old Testament preaching messages of judgment on those who turned their backs on God. God raised up prophets to do that very thing. Jonah was an example.

God told Jonah, "Go to the great city of Ninevah and preach against it, because its wickedness has come up before me" (Jonah 1:1).

God also used prophets to deliver the good news of salvation. Isaiah prophesied about the Messiah approximately 700 years before Jesus' birth.

> For to us a child is born, to us a son is given, and
> the government will be on his shoulders. And
> he will be called Wonderful Counselor, Mighty
> God, Everlasting Father, Prince of Peace. Of the
> increase of his government and peace there will
> be no end. He will reign on David's throne. And
> over his kingdom, establishing and upholding it
> with justice and righteousness from that time on
> and forever. The zeal of the LORD Almighty will
> accomplish this. (Isaiah 9:6-7)

Isaiah lived in Jerusalem. He called the kings, leaders and the people of Israel to faith in God. How appropriate that God would choose a homeboy to give His message that He would be sending the Savior, the Messiah of the world to His people. Isaiah spoke in the present as if it was taking place. "For to us a child **is** born, to us a son **is** given" (emphasis added).

Think about that. Why do you think he spoke in the present about something that would not happen for 700 years?

Isaiah was only speaking the words that God had given him. God had set it in motion, but the physical manifestation would be revealed in the future. Isaiah spoke as if it WAS because it was going to happen. God was saying, "Jesus is coming. Jesus is coming. Your salvation and your hope are coming."

For he spoke, and it came to be; he commanded and it stood firm. (Psalm 33:9)

Jesus would be born, revealed in the physical, when God said ... it's time! Isaiah didn't know when that time would be, but God knew.

In Proverbs 31:1, the words, prophesy or oracle means "word" or "utterance." But there's more. Here it means "what is lifted and carried." It can refer to a physical burden. When used to express a burden or load, it is commonly used to describe that which is placed on the backs of pack animals, like donkeys, mules, or camels. It can also refer to a prophetic utterance.[1]

Allow me to sum it up using the Hebrew meaning. The king's mother taught her son with words that carried with them a burden, lifted up and carried. This momma was burdened for her beloved son. I want you to visualize the burden this mother carried as a heavy weight that an animal would carry on its back.

Speaking from my own experience, there is a difference when you're trying to teach words to your child when you are burdened. In those times, the words used to teach them can vary from speaking with boldness and confidence of the authority over them to down-right pleading with them to do what is right. And believe me, there is a very fine line.

It's amazing how we as parents can rehearse all kinds of speeches (oracles) in our heads that sound so good ... in our heads ... but in reality, the load of the burden we carry can make the words that come from our mouths sound so desperate and urgent.

Can you recall a time this rang true either as a parent or as a child when your parent instructed you from a burdened heart?

_____

_____

We don't know what prompted this instruction from King Lemuel's mother. Was it from her own experience, something from her past maybe that she wanted to make sure wasn't passed down to her son? Or maybe she had seen something in him that told her that he might have weaknesses in certain areas of his life. Whatever the case, she took her role as his parent seriously.

The responsibility and honor that God has given a woman (mother) in her home is an essential role.

Write Proverbs 14:1.

_____

_____

We are home builders! Within our home, we have to, or maybe better said, we get to mold our children's character by teaching them the ways of the Lord and creating an atmosphere of holiness and joy.

Read Psalm 127:1. Under whose leadership are we under in home building?

_____

The queen mother would have been from a Jewish background. Let's see how Rabbi Eliyahu Hoffman describes a typical Jewish home:

> It is indeed the father's role to educate his child in the study of Torah and its laws and ordinances; it is the mother who creates the atmosphere that permeates the very walls of the Jewish home. It is her duty to see to it that the atmosphere be one of Torah [God's teaching, first five books of the Old Testament], kedushah [prayer], and shalom [peace].[2]

What would this home life look like? Picture what would take place. Don't forget to describe attitudes of the parents and children. Be specific.

In reference to Proverbs 1:8 ("Listen, my child, to the rebuke of your father, and do not forsake the Torah of your mother."), the Rabbi goes on to say:

> Observing the attitudes and reactions of a parent
> to the daily hustle and bustle of a Jewish home
> is a far more powerful and influential source of
> education than any lesson learned from a book,
> and it is this "Torah of your mother" to which
> King Solomon refers.[3]

Torah translated often as "law" actually means "teaching."

We have our children under our care for a few short years. Therefore, it's so important to start early in teaching them what it means to honor God in our home. Simple things make a difference, like praying before meals and at bedtime, or memorizing a Bible verse a week. For years, I have watched my daughter-in-law, Nicole, stop at the back door before leaving each morning for prayer with her boys. There are so many powerful ways to show those entrusted to us that God is a priority in our lives.

I think about my granddaughter, Sadie. At twelve months old, we have to watch and wait to see how her personality will develop and what type of learning she will respond to, but the One who made her already knows all that. Therefore, we have to allow Him to guide and direct us in training her to be the God-fearing and God-loving woman He created her to be.

Now what about you? What are some things you are presently doing to show that God is a priority in your home?

_____

_____

Has God revealed something to you that He wants you to do?

_____

_____

Joshua said "Choose for yourselves this day whom you will serve ... as for me and my household, we will serve the LORD" (v. 24:15).

So, I say to you, choose for yourselves that you and your household will serve the Lord, then move forward in training this next generation that the Lord reigns! I promise you, they are listening and watching.

I pray, literally, that my grandsons, Jude and Drew, and our baby, Sadie's, testimony will be: "I took hold of the Lord's hand and heart early in my life. I made the decision to follow Him and to live my life in obedience to His Word. He has been faithful to me. I will continue to love Him and serve Him as He leads me. Amen!"

My desire is to see my children and grandchildren having the determination and perseverance to walk in obedience with the Lord. I believe King Lemuel's mother had the same desire. We will see as we continue in our study that her boldness in mentoring her son came from a heart that was determined to persevere in obedience to her Lord.

Lately, I have been thinking about my circle of friends in this present season. Most are younger than I am by ten to twenty-plus years. God has put these young women in my life. I am very aware of the example that I set before them. I am a spiritual mother to them. They call me or text me asking me to pray for them. They also allow me the privilege of celebrating the victories in their lives. If you do not have children, please know you are a mentor to those around you.

I am aware that there are so many women who long to be mothers, but they are still waiting for their heart's desire: children. For those women, I believe God is supplying that need for now, somehow. I am reminded of Paul and Timothy. 1 Timothy 1:2 says, "To Timothy my true son in the faith." God appointed the two of them to be united, and Paul became Timothy's spiritual father. Paul took that role seriously, loving Timothy and teaching him the ways of the Lord. Timothy was most likely not allowed in synagogue school because his father was a Gentile. This certainly reinforces the investment of his grandmother, Lois, and mother, Eunice, as well as Paul (2 Timothy 1:5).

My daughter, Tiffany, waited painfully for a child. During those years, God supplied her with spiritual daughters whether she realized it or not. They looked to her as an example and sought advice and instruction from her whether they realized it or not. He also sent spiritual mothers to love her and encourage her to continue to move forward one step at a time. In those years of infertility followed by two miscarriages, Tiffany never lost hope even though her heart was broken. It continued to beat because God had a plan that she couldn't see. Although we still don't fully understand the outcome of those days, I see a woman of deeper faith in my beloved child. She thought that dark season was going to literally kill her, but God had more living for her to do. The small ray of hope that God kindled inside her sustained her until He gave her Sadie. I am sure that God will continue to fulfill His plan and purpose for her life.

The words of prophecy that this mother spoke to her son, who belonged to God, were from a burdened heart.

Now take a few minutes to talk to God. Read back through your completed work today and respond to Him.

Lord, help me be Your mouthpiece to my children and/or to those you send me to mentor.

**The sayings of King Lemuel—an oracle
his mother taught him. (Proverbs 31:1)**

Further Study

Look up the verses below and write the one that speaks most
to you today. Psalm 71:17; Proverbs 4:11; Isaiah 54:13; Job 6:24:
Psalm 32:8

_____

_____

Why did you choose that verse?

_____

_____

What is God saying directly to you through that verse?

_____

_____

Pray for God's leadership in teaching your children or those entrusted to you.

ENDNOTES:

[1] James Strong, *The Strongest Strong's Exhaustive Concordance of the Bible*, eds. John R. Kohlenberger and James A. Swanson (Grand Rapids, MI: Zondervan, 2001).

[2] Rabbi Eliyahu Hoffman, "The Jewish Mother—A Hair-Raising Responsibility," Torah.org, March 5, 2003, https://torah.org/torah-portion/olas-shabbos-5763-vayakhel/.

[3] Ibid.

Son, Listen to Me

PROVERBS 31:2

King Lemuel's mother, with a burdened heart, begins to address her son. Read out loud from each translation below. You will hear the words of deep affection this mother has for her son.

KJV	NASB	NIV
What, my son? and what, the son of my womb? and what the son of my vows?	What, O my son? And what, O son of my womb? And what, O son of my vows?	O my son, O son of my womb, O son of my vows.

The repetitions denote earnestness. It's as if she is saying "listen to me." I'm smiling right now because I just had a flashback of a conversation I had with my daughter during her teenage years. She would get so irritated with me because I would repeat myself over and over even within a few minutes of a conversation. I remember one day she said, "Mom, I heard you the first time." My response was, "Tiff, I want you to get this." As parents, we repeat instruction so that we make sure that it is hammered home. I guess the same thing could be accomplished by hypnotizing said child, but I don't know anyone who has used that method. So I, for one, came back to the repetition until there was something in her eyes that told me, "I understand."

In Scripture, God uses repetition. He, as our Father, repeats Himself so that there's no misunderstanding that He means what He says. Keeping that in mind, whenever a word or phrase is repeated in Scripture within a verse or a passage, we would be wise to listen up. After all, God is speaking, right?

What, (O) my son?

"My son," this is a term of special affection. "My child, my boy, you are mine."

Read Isaiah 43:1. Fill in the blanks on the last part of that verse. Remember, this is God speaking. "I have summoned you by name: you _____."

Galatians 3:26 says: "You are all [daughters] of God through faith in Christ Jesus."

What must a person do to have faith in Christ Jesus? Write Romans 10:13.

_____

_____

Now list the steps that one takes to be saved. I have the first one done for you. Read Romans 10:9.
    1. Confess with your mouth that "Jesus is Lord."
    2. _____

For it is with your heart that you believe and are justified,
and it is with your mouth that you confess and are saved.
(Romans 10:10)

By faith in Jesus Christ, God calls you daughter. How does that make you feel?

_____

_____

1 John 3:1 says, "How great is the love the Father has lavished on us, that we should be called the children of God! And that is what we are!"

Because of His great love for His children, He cares for us. Let me say that another way. He takes care of us.

Write Psalm 33:13-15.

_____

_____

Now write Psalm 34:4.

_____

_____

Imagine it, the God who sees all of mankind, watching all who live on earth, also answers our prayers. He delivered King David from all his fears.

Let's look at Daniel, chapter 10 to get some insight about God hearing our prayers and responding. I pray this will fall fresh on you.

Read Daniel 10:10-13. Now focus in on verse 12 and fill in the blanks.

"Do not be afraid, Daniel. Since the _____ day that you set your mind to gain understanding and to _____ yourself before your _____, your words were heard, and I have come in response to them."

Reread the verse above. Daniel's humble heart and a mind set on gaining understanding got God's attention. When our hearts and minds are focused on Him, there's nothing that will stop Him from getting to us. The same One who sends the lightning bolts on their way (Job 38:35) sends us aid when we call out to Him.

Have you considered that God calls out the angels to come to your rescue? God loves you and He responds to your prayers.

Allow me to ask you the same question after looking at this Scripture in Daniel 10.

How does it make you feel to know that your God calls you "my daughter"?

_____

_____

Write Isaiah 49:15.

_____

_____

Like King Lemuel's mother, you and I can't imagine forgetting our children. The compassion that we feel allows us to show mercy and grace to them no matter what their words or actions. God is using this as a measure for us. To me He's saying, "How much more will I **not** forget you. Never, ever will I stop loving you. I am your Creator and God."

and what, the son of my womb?

As a mother who has experienced carrying a child full term I can say without any hesitation that to feel your baby move, kick, or have hiccups from inside your womb is one of the most special times for a momma. For my daughter, as well as many others, it was a stressful time analyzing each moment of her pregnancy, thinking the worst outcome could be possible. Consider this: If Solomon was King Lemuel, then Bathsheba would be the mother in Proverbs 31 addressing her son. While pregnant with him, it would be only natural for her to be stressed from all the "what ifs" because David and Bathsheba's baby born prior to Solomon only lived 7 days (2 Samuel 12:15-24). She became pregnant with Solomon after losing that baby. Solomon would indeed be her beloved son, her "son of my womb."

We can be sure, whether this man was Solomon or not, this mother had a "heart connection" with her son. While pregnant with him, she had experienced it all, leg cramps during the night, hanging over the toilet with morning sickness, and should we even speak of the mood swings from raging hormones? He was the beloved child who grew inside her as she carried him under her heart.

and what (O) the son of my vows?

Vowing was a voluntary action, but it was very serious; therefore, it was to be made only after careful consideration.

> If you make a vow to the LORD your God, do not
> be slow to pay it, for the LORD your God will
> certainly demand it of you and you will be guilty
> of sin. But if you refrain from making a vow,
> you will not be guilty. Whatever your lips utter
> you must be sure to do, because you made your
> vow freely to the LORD your God with your own
> mouth. (Deuteronomy 23:21–24)

> When a man [or woman] makes a vow to the
> LORD or takes an oath to obligate himself by a
> pledge, he must not break his word but must do
> everything he said. (Numbers 30:2)

Hannah's vow to the Lord immediately comes to my mind.

> She [Hannah] made a vow, saying, "O LORD Al-
> mighty, if you will only look upon your servant's
> misery and remember me, and not forget your
> servant but give her a son, then I will give him to
> the LORD for all the days of his life, and no razor
> will ever be used on his head."(1 Samuel 1:11)

And there were others who made vows.

> Jacob made a vow, saying, "If God will be with
> me and will watch over me on this journey I am
> taking and will give me food to eat and clothes to
> wear so that I return safely to my father's house,
> then the LORD will be my God and this stone that
> I have set up as a pillar will be God's house, and
> of all that you give me I will give you a tenth."
> (Genesis 28:20–22)

Israel made this vow to the Lord:

"If you will deliver these people into our hands, we will totally destroy their cities. The LORD listened to Israel's plea and gave the Canaanites over to them. They completely destroyed them and their towns." (Numbers 21:2–3)

Jephthah made a vow to the Lord:

"If you give the Ammonites into my hands, whatever comes out of the door of my house to meet me when I return in triumph from the Ammonites will be the LORD's, and I will sacrifice it as a burnt offering." (Judges 11:30–31)

It's as if to say, "Lord, if you will do this for me, then I will do this...."

The one word that comes to my mind when I think about King Lemuel's mother making vows to the Lord is deliberate. There's no doubt that she is devout in her faith. This mother knew the sacredness of her vows. I feel her saying, "Son, I take my vows to God seriously and you have to also." She had carefully thought out how she would address her son because I believe that she had considered carefully and fully what her relationship with God would be.

We will see as we continue in this study that the queen mother's fear of the Lord was her driving force in all that she did. Her relationship with Him was due to the steadfast dependency that she had on Him. Our spiritual maturity has everything to do with the measure of our dependence we have on Him. Jesus said:

"Let the little children come to me, and do not hinder them, for the kingdom of God belongs to such as these. I tell you the truth, anyone who will not receive the kingdom of God like a little child will never enter it." (Luke 18:16–17)

Jesus is talking about being deliberate in our dependence on Him.

Little children, babies like our Sadie, rely on their parents or caregivers to supply all their needs. As long as their basic needs are met, they are content. They are totally dependent on someone else. They grow into the toddler stage and take those first steps. Although still dependent, they slowly begin to taste the independence that awaits them. As they mature physically, they pull away from the dependency on their parents and their sin nature kicks in.

Life as a teenager brings rebellion (do I hear an AMEN?) and a much bigger dose of independence. As the adult years are ushered in, we often live on overdrive with massive amounts of responsibilities and expectations placed on us by ourselves and others. Rebellion can continue from lack of self-control, discipline, or ignorance because, quite frankly, we don't know any better. We live our lives the best we know how with stress and anxiety in control.

With physical growth, independence matures, yet the opposite holds true in the spiritual realm. Jesus says spiritual maturity is based on dependence, not independence. "'Come, follow me' Jesus said, 'and I will make you fishers of men,'" (Matthew 4:19). He also said, "Come to me, all you who are weary and burdened, and I will give you rest. Take my yoke [teaching] upon you and learn from me, for I am gentle and humble in heart, and you will find rest for your souls" (Matthew 11:28–29).

The key is dependency upon Him. The question is this: How do we develop this childlike dependency? Let's look back at Luke 18:16–17:

> But Jesus called the children to him and said, "Let the little children come to me, and do not hinder them, for the kingdom of God belongs to such as these. I tell you the truth, anyone who will not receive the kingdom of God like a little child will never enter it."

Jesus said this is the truth, tested and approved, anyone, meaning all, who will not receive... I have to stop there.

The Greek word for receive means to "welcome," "receive," "accept," and "take." Two words from the Greek meaning that I want to focus on are welcome and take.[1]

Welcome means to receive it without hesitation and with gladness. The word take suggests receiving it deliberately. I believe that Jesus is saying to us that to have childlike dependency, you have to be deliberate in receiving it.

Deliberate according to *The American Heritage Dictionary* means "considered or planned in advance with a full awareness of everything involved."[2]

Have you considered or planned in advance with a full awareness of everything involved as to where you are right now in your relationship with Him? Is that relationship maturing?

Can you hear His voice clearer in this present season than you could a year ago? Can you hear that call to be deliberate? Tough questions, I know, but Jesus says that we have to be deliberate as it relates to our relationship with Him.

You see, King Lemuel's mother was deliberate because she knew in whom she believed. Her Source was steadfast and true. He had given her a son. He was her gift, and she was his honored mother, responsible for the vows she made. Being true to herself and her God was the only way. She had no other choice.

Take a few minutes to pray, asking God to show you how dependent you are on Him right now. Ask Him to help you give every area of your life to Him, holding back nothing so that your dependency is His and His alone.

There's one last aspect that we need to explore with the making of vows.

Look up Proverbs 20:25 and write it below:

_____

_____

Now, write Psalm 66:13–14.

_____

_____

Why do you think God gives us the warning in Proverbs 20:25? (Hint: Psalm 66:13–14)

_____

_____

Each of the Scripture examples that we looked at earlier of those making vows in the Bible (Genesis 28:20, Numbers 21:2-3, Judges 11:30-31, 1 Samuel 1:11, 2 Samuel 15:7-8) were in desperate need for the Lord's help.

Let's look at one more:

> "In my distress I called to the LORD, and he answered me. From the depths of the grave I called for help, and you listened to my cry." (Jonah 2:2)

> "But I, with a song of thanksgiving, will sacrifice to you. What I have vowed I will make good. 'Salvation comes from the LORD.'" And the LORD commanded the fish, and it vomited Jonah onto dry land. (Jonah 2:9–10)

That's another example of "vows my lips promised and my mouth spoke when I was in trouble" (Psalm 66:14). We can understand better why God wants us to consider our vows wisely so that we won't dedicate something rashly (Proverbs 20:25) because that is a trap from the enemy.

King Lemuel was a beloved son. He was also a son that came to his mother through a promise to God.

Lord, help me be deliberate about my dependency upon you.

_____

_____

_____

_____

**O my son, O son of my womb, O son of my vows.
(Proverbs 31:2)**

Further Study

Read the entire section on Jephthah, Judges 11–12:1–10. I realize that it's a lot to read, but it will be so worth the extra time.

Write the vow Jephthah made to the Lord. Read Judges 11:30-31.

_____

_____

Would this be the kind of vow Proverbs 20:25 speaks of?

_____

Who came out of Jephthah's house upon his arrival from battle? Read Judges 11:34.

_____

What was the outcome of fulfilling his vow? Read Judges 11:35–39.

_____

_____

Vows were serious. Reread Deuteronomy 23:21–23.

Endnotes:
[1]James Strong, *The Strongest Strong's Exhaustive Concordance of the Bible*, eds. John R. Kohlenberger and James A. Swanson (Grand Rapids, MI: Zondervan, 2001).
[2]*The American Heritage Dictionary*, 2nd College Ed.,s.v. "deliberate."

Beware, My Son

In our study, we are now entering the instruction that King Lemuel's mother gives him about potential sin that can easily entangle him.

KJV	NASB	NIV
Give not thy strength unto women, nor thy ways to that which destroyeth kings.	Do not give your strength to women, or your ways to that which destroys kings.	Do not spend your strength on women, your vigor on those who ruin kings.

The writer of Hebrews speaks of sin and how it can entangle us. Write Hebrews 12:1 starting with:
Let us throw off everything that hinders and the

_____

_____

In Hebrews 12:1, the writer wants us to envision our life as if we are in a race, running one foot in front of the other toward Jesus, eyes fixed and feet steady in life's race. When we give way to sin, it will trip us every time.

Allow me to share how God spoke to me about sin while gardening. One Saturday last spring, the weather was unusually perfect. The sky was as blue as the ocean and the cool breeze balanced the heat from the brightly shining sun. My husband, Oatman, had set his sights on yardwork. He climbed on his trusty John Deere and began mowing. Hearing the growl of the mower from inside the house, guilt set in. "I should go do some weeding," I thought. This was a huge sacrifice on my part because I dislike yardwork. Women who spend days working in their yards are my heroes. I wish I could love it, but I don't.

But to be the wife that I so want to be, I begrudgingly dragged myself outside to pull weeds. I waved at Oatman so he would notice me being such a workhorse. I took a deep breath and begin ripping those weeds, roots and all, out of the ground. The weeds I noticed had taken over my beautiful purple irises. Some of the weeds were so easy to remove. Others were a bit stubborn, but with a little more determination on my part, I managed to yank handfuls out of the ground. Others, no matter how much I yanked and pulled, refused to dislodge themselves from the grip that held their roots tightly in place. Oatman, noticing that I was struggling, stopped the mower and walked over to help me. I had been in conversation with God during this time, so I seized the opportunity to share with him as he took over. "These weeds are like our sin nature," I began. He laughed as I continued to share with him what my conversation with God had been. This is what God spoke into my heart and what I shared with my man.

The weeds that were easily pulled from the ground represent the sin that is not repeated. In other words, it's not a stronghold in your life. Let me give you an example. It was the year of 1979, my senior year at Murray High School, when friends approached me one day about skipping school. I had never skipped school. My friends reasoned that we would not miss any classes. They promised that we would only be gone during our lunch period. After much persuasion, I agreed to go with them to the Dairy Queen. I was miserable the whole way there. Back in those days, no one was permitted to leave school unless it was due to sickness or a family emergency—not even during lunch. Anyway, once at the "DQ," we jumped quickly out of the car to get in line. While in line to order, I turned around to see my mother in her car right in front of me, stopped in traffic. I was horrified! I honestly didn't know if she had spotted me or not.

We walked back into the school with no repercussions from the school administrators. But that didn't matter because I had already been caught. My stomach was in one big knot for the rest of the day. I anticipated my mother's arrival home from work and met her at the door with a full confession. To my surprise, she was a good sport about the whole thing. She laughed and gave me a kiss on my cheek. Yes, you guessed it, she had not seen me. As she walked away, still laughing, her words were "don't do it again." And I never did. God sometimes says to us after a particular sin, "don't do it again" and we don't. It's like a weed that comes out so easily. We are not even tempted to repeat that particular sin.

Has any sin come to mind for you?

_____

_____

Then there's the sin that is a bit tougher to lay aside. Conviction comes and we are determined not to repeat it, only to be convicted again of the same sin. I don't know what this is or has been in your life. For some it may be the lack of respect for their husband or yelling at their children because of lack of patience from a bad day. For others, it may be drinking too much or using language that destroys their witness. It's a different sin for different people, and it represents the weed that is tougher to yank out.

Oatman gave the third kind of weed his full strength. He pulled and tugged. He even divided it into sections, readjusting his grip and continued to pull with all his might, finally dislodging it from the ground. He said, "It's deep-rooted."

"Wow! Honey, that'll preach," I responded. Some of our sin nature is deep-rooted, isn't it? It's a stronghold in our life. Over and over again it slaps us in the face, and we allow it. Two of mine come to mind right away, the sins of worry and fear. Only through the strength of our Gardener can a stronghold of deep-rooted sin be uprooted and discarded once and for all.

Oatman smiled as he got back on the mower. Secretly, I knew that he loved playing the part of the Father. I squealed out, raised my hands toward the heavens and shouted, "Praise Jesus." It's a good thing our nearest neighbor is down the road a ways. They might have come out on their porch to see what the dogs were barking about.

What sin has taken root in your life?

Have you felt the process of the Lord yanking, pulling, and pluck-
ing out that sin? Explain.

_____

_____

I loved my teaching lesson that day. The Lord and I had such a
great time. I am a visual learner, so I am always thankful for any
visual aids He provides.

The beautiful purple irises can be easily taken over by the
weeds. We also can be so easily taken over by our sin nature. Our
Lord is and will always be faithful in uprooting it. The following
morning after my gardening session, I could hardly move. I had
obviously pulled muscles in my lower back. I was reminded that
God's weeding can be very painful. I realize more and more that
we have to experience pain to build within us the character of
Christ. Because of the great disease of sin, God spends our lifetime breaking us free of what comes natural to us in our flesh to
what will free us in His Spirit.

Remember, we are a work in progress on this earth.

In Proverbs 31:3, the king's mother warned her son about
women. It's important for us to recall that in the royal courts, life
was different than what we would picture it to be. It was certainly not uncommon for kings to have lots of women. We see in the
Book of Esther that Esther was only one of the virgins brought
to the palace to be under the care of Hegai, the king's eunuch.
Scripture says that Hegai was in charge of the women, the harem.

The word harem actually means "house of the women." The
"house of the women" spent their days with beauty treatments

to prepare for a night with the king. They waited, each one to be summoned for their time, then sent back not knowing when or if he would call for them again.

Read Esther 2:14.

Esther had been queen, married to the king for five years when she told Mordecai, her cousin, that it had been thirty days since the king had summoned her (Esther 4:11).

I think you get the picture. How sad.

Do not spend your strength on women,
Strength here means power, valor, and virtue.[1] "Don't be tripped up, entangled in sin", I feel the queen mother saying. "It will drain your power and take your valor and virtue."

Think harem here, lots of women! We see in Scripture that kings had wives and concubines, which made up their harems. Concubines were wives of secondary rank.

Let's explore this in the Word.

> After he left Hebron, David took more concu-
> bines and wives in Jerusalem, and more sons and
> daughters were born to him. (2 Samuel 5:13)

> The king set out, with his entire household fol-
> lowing him; but he left ten concubines to take
> care of the palace. (2 Samuel 15:16)

By this verse we know that King David had at least ten concubines.

He [Solomon] had seven hundred wives of royal birth and three hundred concubines, and his wives led him astray. (1 Kings 11:3)

Rehoboam loved Maacah daughter of Absalom more than any of his other wives and concubines. In all, he had eighteen wives and sixty concubines, twenty-eight sons and sixty daughters. (2 Chronicles 11:21)

Sixty queens there may be, and eighty concubines, and virgins beyond number. (Song of Songs 6:8)

your vigor on those who ruin kings.
In 1 Kings 11:3, Scripture says that Solomon's wives led him astray. How?

See 1 Kings 11:4-10.

_____

_____

Use your imagination. In what other ways could the "house of women" ruin kings?

_____

_____

How could one woman cause a king to do something he wouldn't have done ordinarily? Read Mark 6:14–29.

_____

_____

> My son, give me your heart and let your eyes
> keep to my ways, for a prostitute is a deep pit and
> a wayward wife is a narrow well. Like a bandit
> she lies in wait, and multiplies the unfaithful
> among men. (Proverbs 23:26–28)

In this culture, kings would have had many women, but we also know that it only takes one to turn a man away from the ways of the Lord. That would have caused his ruin.

King Lemuel's mother warned him against women who could ruin him. Remember, King Lemuel belonged to God.

Lord, may I be a woman after your own heart, committed to You foremost, then committed to

_____

_____

**Do not spend your strength on women, your vigor
on those who ruin kings. (Proverbs 31:3)**

Further Study

Samson and Delilah: read Judges 16:4–30.

Scripture tells us that Samson fell in love with Delilah. Based on Delilah's actions, do you think she felt the same about Samson?

_____

_____

What did Delilah have to gain by Samson's destruction? Judges 16:5

_____

_____

What happened to Samson? Judges 16:23–30

_____

_____

Was Delilah a woman who had her husband's best interest in mind or her own?

_____

_____

King Lemuel's mother said, "Beware, my son!"

Endnotes:
[1]James Strong, *The Strongest Strong's Exhaustive Concordance of the Bible,* eds. John R. Kohlenberger and James A. Swanson (Grand Rapids, MI: Zondervan, 2001).

Not You, King

PROVERBS 31:4

Today we continue our study on the warnings from Lemuel's mother. Yesterday we explored the first warning in verse 3: "Do not spend your strength on women: your vigor on those who ruin kings" (Proverbs 31:3).

KJV	NASB	NIV
This is not for kings, O Lemuel, it is not for kings to drink wine, nor for princes strong drink.	It is not for kings, O Lemuel, it is not for kings to drink wine, or for rulers to desire strong drink.	It is not for kings, O Lemuel—not for kings to drink wine, not for rulers to crave beer.

It is obvious from verses 3 and 4 that his mother is teaching him about purity from two different sins, uncleanness and drunkenness. Either could destroy him.

I want us to look at a passage of Scripture found in John 8:1–11. You don't have to turn there, just picture the scene as I relay it to you.

One day all the people had gathered around Jesus in the temple courts. He sat down and began to teach them. His Bible study was interrupted by the teachers of the law and the Pharisees.

They had brought Him a woman caught in the act of adultery. I would envision that they had both of her arms, thrusting her toward Jesus. Maybe she fell as the people stared at her. The religious leaders were intent on embarrassing her, mocking her sin in public. And not just in public but at the temple where God's holy presence resided. No doubt they were demeaning and cruel, and Scripture says they used this time to try to trap Jesus.

The *Believer's Bible Commentary* says this:

> They wanted the Lord to contradict the Law of Moses. If they could succeed in doing that, then they could turn the common people against Jesus. They reminded the Lord that Moses, in the law, commanded that a person caught in the act of adultery should be stoned to death. For their own wicked purposes, the Pharisees hoped the Lord would disagree, and so they asked Him what he had to say on the subject. They thought that justice and the Law of Moses demanded that she should be made an example.[1]

I wonder how the crowd of people reacted to the scene. Maybe they stood quiet, or maybe they whispered to one another, sizing up this woman who had been caught in the act of her sin.

Jesus leaned down and wrote something in the dirt. In this passage of Scripture, it doesn't tell us what Jesus wrote, although my pastor recently pointed out to me the following verse in Jeremiah.

> O LORD, the hope of Israel, all who forsake you will be put to shame. Those who turn away from

you will be written in the dust because they have
forsaken the LORD, the spring of living water.
(Jeremiah 17:13)

The teachers of the law and Pharisees would have known this
passage well. Jesus could have been writing their names one by
one in the dirt. That would have certainly gotten their attention.

We do know that years before, on a mountain, God wrote on
stone tablets "You shall not commit adultery" as part of the Ten
Commandments.

These are the commands the LORD proclaimed in
a loud voice to your whole assembly there on the
mountain from out of the fire, the cloud and the
deep darkness; and he added nothing more. Then
He wrote them on two stone tablets and gave
them to [Moses]. (Deuteronomy 5:22)

I love how the Word assures us that God spoke with passion
as He proclaimed to the whole assembly in a loud voice, as if to
say, "Don't miss this people! Hear me say this; do not commit
adultery!" Then He wrote it so that generations to come would
know His proclamation. Jesus said in Matthew 5:17: "Do not
think that I come to abolish the Law or the Prophets; I have not
come to abolish them but to fulfill them."

God's Law is God's teachings. His teachings tell us how we are
to live our lives. Jesus is the fulfillment of the Law and prophets
because His life reflected the teachings of God perfectly. Jesus
fulfilled the Law because He is perfection, and He is our perfect
example of how we are to live. What the people gathered around
the temple saw that day was the living breathing Law of God.

After writing on the ground with His finger, Jesus straightened up as the teachers and Pharisees continued questioning Him. Then He spoke. "If any one of you is without sin, let him be the first to throw a stone at her" (John 8:7). Jesus' response was not about the Law itself but about who should be the one to carry it out. Would it have been right for other sinners to throw stones? Jesus broke through hearts that day as one by one the people walked away. The Bible tells us that the only two remaining were Jesus and the woman. Only minutes before, the woman faced a very real possibility of physical death, but Jesus had delivered her. "Woman, where are they? Has no one condemned you?" Then showing her great mercy out of His grace, Jesus said, "Then neither do I condemn you" (John 8: 10–11).

The Greek word used here for condemn is *katakrino*, meaning "to judge against." Jesus chose mercy instead of judgment.[2]

Jesus gave her a new start. He said, "Go now and leave your life of sin" (John 8:11). Jesus gave her the opportunity to see her sin and the way it was taking her. Then, face-to-face with the Law, she saw the love of God (deep sigh) ... amazing grace!

It is not for kings, O Lemuel—not for kings to drink wine, not for rulers to crave beer,

King Lemuel's mother knew the love of God. I believe her son knew this love also. How could he test that love? His mother with her burdened heart said to her son, "This sin that could easily entangle you is not for you."

What are some of the effects of too much alcohol on the body?
See Isaiah 28:7 and Proverbs 23:29-35.

_____

_____

How could too much alcohol ruin a man?

_____

_____

How could it ruin a king?

_____

_____

Our sin nature is ugly, and it's different sin for different people. Some struggle with the sin of adultery; others struggle with selfishness or a bad temper, but all are ugly and destructive.

A few weeks ago I pulled up to a stoplight to turn right. The light was red. I stopped and waited for the steady flow of cars to pass. The second that there was a break in the traffic, the driver in the car behind me started honking at me to go. It startled me, so I looked in my rearview mirror to see an agitated woman behind the wheel. By that time, my window of opportunity to pull out had passed. This did not make the woman happy one bit. I tried my hardest to ignore her and wait for the light to turn. The second the light turned green, she began honking her horn again. Honestly, my brain had just told me that the light was green. Her brain had told her the light is green, she's still not pulling out, so you better let her know you're angry over her stupidity. I think her brain waves were sharper than mine, don't you?

I pulled out quickly because, quite frankly, I was afraid not to. She was right behind me, but quickly made her break. I watched her swerve in and out of the traffic ahead of me. I thought to myself, there must be some type of emergency, or maybe this woman is just out of control. The next stoplight had traffic stopped. As I approached the light turning left, I chuckled to myself. This time I was behind her. We both turned into the same shopping center. You may be surprised to find out that she wasn't going to a fire or the hospital. She was going to the grocery store. Now, I know that I didn't know her situation. Maybe her blood sugar had dropped and she needed some food quickly. But, I suspect that it wasn't any type of emergency. I suspect the woman behind the wheel of that car was out of control. Life was not going her way, and she acted out. Or better said, "She acted ugly," as my mother would say.

Oh, and just so we are all on the same page, the Bible says that "all have sinned and fall short of the glory of God" (Romans 3:23).

Write Romans 3:10.

_____

_____

Write Isaiah 53:6.

_____

_____

The king's mother was warning him because this direction in life, women and alcohol, was not what God wanted for him. God had a great purpose for his life. She had talked to God about her son. She knew that God would be faithful to fulfill His promises, and she was deliberate in fulfilling her promises to God concerning her son. Now, from a burdened heart, she was warning her son to turn away from sin, to become the man and king God had created him to be.

Write Ephesians 5:18.

_____

_____

Definition of debauchery: 1. Extreme indulgence of one's appetites; dissipation. 2. (plural) orgies. 3. a leading astray morally.[3]

Read Galatians 5:19-21.

In this list of the acts of the sinful nature, which ones could destroy a king, especially one who belonged to God? Explain your answer.

_____

_____

The opposite of the acts of the sinful nature would be the Fruit of the Spirit. Galatians 5:22–23. They are:

_____

_____

_____

_____

Write Galatians 5:24–25

_____

_____

The king's mother knew possibly that alcohol was a weakness along with women. She also knew too much of both could ruin him. This mother is directing her son in the ways of the Lord, to walk in the Spirit, not by a sinful nature.

Lord, I thank You that because I belong to You, my sinful nature has been crucified. Help me live my life in step with the Spirit.

_____

_____

It is not for kings, O Lemuel—not for kings to drink wine, not for rulers to crave beer. (Proverbs 31:4)

Further Study:

Read Genesis 19:30–38.
This Scripture covers the ill effects of women and alcohol.

What did Lot's older daughter plot? Why?

_____

_____

How was the plan carried out? (vv. 33-35)

_____

_____

What was the outcome of their sin against their father?

_____

_____

King Lemuel's mother said, "It's not for kings to drink wine or beer, O Lemuel!!"

ENDNOTES:
[1]William MacDonald, *Believer's Bible Commentary*, ed. Arthur L. Farstad (Nashville: Thomas Nelson, 2016).
[2]James Strong, *Expanded Edition Strong's Complete Word Study Concordance*, ed. Warren Baker (Chattanooga, TN: AMG Publishers, 2004).
[3]*Webster's New World Dictionary*, Concise Ed., s.v. "debauchery."

Remember God's Laws

PROVERBS 31:5

66 **I**t is not for kings, O Lemuel—not for kings to drink wine, not for rulers to crave beer." (Proverbs 31:4)

Let's look to verse 5 to see the explanation to her son.

They can't do it:

KJV	NASB	NIV
Lest they drink, and forget the law, and pervert the judgment of any of the afflicted.	For they will drink and forget what is decreed, and pervert the rights of all the afflicted.	Lest they drink and forget what has been decreed, and deprive all the oppressed of their rights.

Lest they drink and forget what the law decrees

If you left off forgetfulness in the listing of the effects of too much alcohol, make a mental note now.

I came across the following commentary from *The Reformation Study Bible* (New King James Version):

Scripture shows that God intends His law [teachings] to function in three ways....

Its first function is to be a mirror reflecting to us both the perfect righteousness of God and our own sinfulness and shortcomings.... The law is meant to give knowledge of sin (Rom. 3:20; 4:15; 5:13; 7:7-11), and by showing us our need of pardon and our danger of damnation to lead us in repentance and faith to Christ (Gal. 3:19-24).

A second function, the "civil use," is to restrain evil. Though the law cannot change the heart, it can to some extent inhibit lawlessness by its threats of judgment, especially when backed by a civil code that administers punishment for proven offenses ... Thus, it secures civil order, and serves to protect the righteous from the unjust.

Its third function is to guide the regenerate into the good works that God has planned for them (Eph. 2:10). The law tells God's children what will please their heavenly Father. It could be called their family code. Christ was speaking of this third use of the law when He said that those who become His disciples must be taught to do all that He had commanded (Matt. 28:20), and that obedience to His commands will prove the reality of one's love for Him (John 14:15). The Christian is free from the law as a system of salvation (Rom. 6:14; 7:4, 6: 1 Cor. 9:20; Gal. 2:15-19; 3:25), but is "under law toward Christ" as a rule of life (1 Cor. 9:21; Gal 6:2).[1]

God's teachings are the ultimate foundation for our direction, provision, and protection. When we stay within the boundaries of His teachings, we can be sure His sovereign covering is over us.

Write John 14:21.

_____

_____

What does our obedience to God's teachings prove to Him?

_____

_____

What does Deuteronomy 6:5 and Matthew 22:37 tell us about how to love God?

_____

_____

Our obedience to what He commands is directly tied to how God sees our love for Him. How does knowing this change your heart toward walking in total obedience to God?

_____

_____

The king had responsibilities as a leader over his kingdom. His mother, as a devout believer, knew the only way for her son to be that leader was to be a follower of the Most High, the King of kings. Only then could he distinguish between right and wrong.

Read 1 Kings 3:1-15 and answer the following questions.

What did God say to Solomon? (v. 5)

_____

_____

What did Solomon want from God? (vv. 7–9)

_____

_____

What does Solomon's prayer tell us about the condition of his heart?

_____

_____

We can be sure that the condition of his heart was righteous because the Lord was pleased (v. 10). (Sadly, later in Solomon's life the condition of his heart changed as we have already studied. 1 Kings 11:3–10).

How did God respond to Solomon's request? (vv.12–15)

_____

_____

God gave him what he asked for. Solomon asked for wisdom and God poured it on him BIG TIME plus added both riches and honor.

What is godly wisdom?

_____

_____

Why is wisdom so important?

_____

_____

"Blessed is the man who finds wisdom, the man who gains understanding." (Proverbs 3:13)

According to *Nelson's New Illustrated Bible Dictionary*, wisdom is the "ability to judge correctly and to follow the best course of action, based on knowledge and understanding."[2]

What will wisdom save you from? Make a list from Proverbs 2:12–15.

_____

_____

What else does having wisdom save you from?

_____

_____

And deprive (pervert) all the oppressed (afflicted) of their rights.

We can certainly understand how too much alcohol clouds a mind and senses. Alcohol would hinder a king from making righteous decisions concerning the oppressed or anyone else for that matter.

Besides alcohol, what else can keep us from seeing the needs of others?

_____

_____

Your list might have included selfishness, distraction, worry, and fear. All of these are obstacles that keep us from obedience.

King Lemuel's mother knew that any temptation that led him to disobey the Word of God had to be removed from his life. The king must put aside evil desires to walk with the Spirit.

Years ago, while on a business trip. I prayed for God to give me an opportunity to be a witness for Him. He didn't waste any time answering my request. On my plane ride home, the man who barely got on before takeoff was God's answer to me. He was out of breath when he sat down in the seat beside me.

After a few minutes he spoke. We had a brief conversation before I pulled out a book about my Savior and settled in for the ride home. I had only read a page or two when the man's attention came back to me. "That looks like a good book," he said. The title of the book gave away the contents. "It is!" I answered. Immediately, the Holy Spirit impressed these words on me, "Ask him if he knows Me."

WHOA!!! Fear rose up in me right away. Silently, I proceeded to give the Lord all the reasons that this question would not be a good idea. Finally, I looked toward the man and found him sleeping. Whew! Silently I said, "Lord, look, he's asleep."

As if the man was hearing my thoughts, his eyes sprang open. Keeping my head looking straight as if I were still reading, I could see him looking at the cover of my book. Again, the Holy Spirit impressed on me, "Ask him if he knows Me." Well, sad to say I let my fear win out. I never asked him. But the story doesn't end there.

The plane landed, we said our goodbyes and exited the plane. I felt horrible as I headed toward the baggage claim area. On the way, I met up with Oatman. We arrived at the baggage claim and were catching up on each other's week, so I hadn't noticed that everyone had gotten their luggage and left except for me and the man. I looked up and there he stood on the other side of the conveyer belt. He waved and smiled. The Holy Spirit for the third time said, "Ask him if he knows Me." I chose not to be obedient.

At the moment my decision was made, our bags came out. As we grabbed our luggage, we waved goodbye and left the airport. On the way home from Nashville, I relayed the story to Oatman and bawled my eyes out.

I still pray for that man from time to time. My heart is so tender approximately twelve years later. The Lord went to great lengths to give me another chance. He even sent the angel troops to sit on our luggage so that all the people would be cleared out except for the two (well ... and Oatman) who had a divine appointment that day.

Disobedience can cost us so much. In some cases, it can alter a person's life for the rest of their life.

> Whoever has my commands and obeys them, he
> is the one who loves me. He who loves me will
> be loved by my Father, and I too will love him
> and show myself to him. (John 14:21)

The queen said, "Son, remember God's law and how to rule your kingdom as such."

King Lemuel's mother wanted her son to live a life of total obedience to the Lord. Through his obedience, others would be taken care of.

Lord, help me be obedient to your commands.

Lest they drink and forget what the law decrees and deprive all the oppressed of their rights. (Proverbs 31:5)

We will do this activity today instead of Further Study.

Before moving to verse 6, think about what kind of vow this mother could have made to God concerning her son. Go back and review verses 1 through 5. Jot down any ideas you have.

_____

_____

Write out a vow that the queen mother might have made to the Lord.

_____

_____

At this point in our study, do you see why our king's mother might be burdened for her son? Explain your answer.

_____

_____

This morning at worship service, I overheard a woman in the pew in front of me ask her adult son to follow her to the altar. Once at the altar, the rest of the family joined them. They were huddled together while the mother prayed. Tears filled my eyes because of the burden this mother had for her son. A mother's heart is tender toward her children no matter the age. I hope her son saw what I saw: A mother escorting her beloved son to the throne room of the Almighty, asking the Father for something on his behalf. Now picture the heavenly realm with Jesus seated at God's right hand, interceding on her behalf. All I can say is that precious woman knows where her help comes from ... "the Maker of heaven and earth" (Psalm 121:2).

ENDNOTES:

[1]*The Reformation Study Bible* (NKJV), ed. R.C. Sproul (Sanford, FL: Reformation Trust Publishing, 2016), http://www.ligonier.org/blog/threefold-use-law/.

[2]*Nelson's New Illustrated Bible Dictionary*, ed. Ronald F. Youngblood (Nashville: Thomas Nelson,1995).

For Others, Not for Kings

PROVERBS 31:6

It's interesting to see that the queen mother warned her son about women in one verse but her warning concerning alcohol is in four. Could alcohol have been his greatest weakness? Certainly could be something to consider.

KJV	NASB	NIV
Give strong drink unto him that is ready to perish, and wine unto those that be of heavy hearts.	Give strong drink to him who is perishing and wine to him whose life is bitter.	Give beer to those who are perishing, wine to those who are in anguish.

We are seeing that King Lemuel's mother not only cares about her son, but she cares about others as well. Her son is not perishing or in anguish, but she knows others who are.

Give strong drink (liquor; beer) to those who are perishing,

The Hebrew meaning of the word perishing is "fading away of strength, hope, wisdom, knowledge, and wealth"[1] as unto death.

Do you know of anyone who is suffering because they are fading away of strength, hope, wisdom, knowledge, and wealth unto death?

Today during Tuesday morning Bible study, a precious saint walked through the doors using a cane for assistance. I could tell by the look in her eyes that the physical pain she was enduring was agonizing. It broke my heart, but I found myself rejoicing secretly with the Lord because the love she has for God's Word not only brought her to class but will also carry her through this difficult time.

I did not serve alcohol to the ladies this morning who gathered for our time of study, (we did have some strong coffee though) because—praise be to God—in today's time we have medicine to aid in healing and help ease the pain of suffering. But, in Biblical times, many in pain would find relief with alcohol. I know what you're thinking; even in modern times many choose alcohol to relieve suffering. Hold that thought; we will get back to it in our next lesson.

Here are some examples in Scripture of alcohol being used for medicine.

In 1 Timothy 5:23, the Apostle Paul said to Timothy:

Stop drinking only water, and use a little wine because of your stomach and your frequent illnesses.

In the story of the Good Samaritan, we see that he took pity on a man who had fallen into the hands of robbers. They had stripped him of his clothes and beaten him, leaving him half dead.

[The Samaritan] went to him and bandaged his wounds, pouring on oil and wine. (Luke 10:34)

Alcohol, as medicine, was used to drink and also as an antiseptic.

Dr. Salvatore P. Lucia, a former professor of medicine at the University of California School of Medicine, wrote, "Wine is the most ancient dietary beverage and the most important medicinal agent in continuous use throughout the history of mankind.... Few other substances available to man have been as widely recommended for their curative powers as have wines."[2]

wine to those who are in anguish (of heavy hearts; deep depression).

I want to focus on the KJV using "heavy hearts." The Hebrew word mara, meaning "bitter" is what you see here for heavy.[1] For heart, think "all that is within a person." The king's mother is saying, "Son, give wine to those whose hearts have lost hope and have become bitter. They are living in anguish."

Read Ruth 1:18–21.

What did Naomi call herself to the women of Bethlehem?_____

Life had been hard in Moab for Naomi. She had endured much suffering and lost hope. "Call me Bitter," she said.

Have you ever been there? Explain.

_____

_____

A few seasons in my life stick out to me right now. I could have easily said, "Don't call me Kathy, call me Bitter."

What are some of the reasons people lose their hope?

_____

_____

What does it mean to hope in the Lord?

_____

_____

Read David's Psalm 62 (it's only 12 verses, so don't cheat—read it all) then fill in the appropriate blanks.

My soul finds _____ in God alone; my _____ comes from him. (v. 1)

He alone is my _____ and my salvation; he is my fortress, I will never be shaken. (v. 2)

Find rest, O my soul, in God alone; my _____ comes from him. (v. 5)

Trust in him at all times, O people; pour out your _____ to him, for God is our _____. (v. 8)

King David knew God was his hope, rest, joy, and righteousness. It was only through Him that David could rule as king, knowing God would supply everything he needed to care for others.

King Lemuel was ruler of his kingdom. His mother wanted him to care for those who were hurting. In fact, it was his responsibility. There were then and are now multitudes of those suffering. We all have times of suffering. Many endure the kind of suffering I can't begin to fathom. It's hard to understand why things happen as they do. Turn with me to the book of Job.

The Bible tells us that Job was blameless and upright, that he feared the Lord and shunned evil. But there was a time of testing for Job that resulted in great loss for him.

Read Job 1:14-19 and fill in the blanks.

What information did the messengers bring to Job?

1st Messenger (Job 1:14–15)

_____

_____

2nd Messenger (Job 1:16)

_____

_____

3rd Messenger (Job 1:17)

_____

_____

4th Messenger (Job 1:18–19)

_____

_____

In verse 20, we see Job's condition after these things took place: He got up, tore his robe and shaved his head. Job was responding externally by tearing his robe and shaving his head to what he was feeling internally: deep grief and despair.

Then he fell to the ground in worship. (Job 1:20)

What happened to Job next, his second time of testing? See Job 2:7–8.

_____

_____

In verse 9, his wife added to his suffering. How?

_____

_____

Write Hebrews 5:7–8.

_____

_____

_____

Jesus learned obedience from what He suffered.

Write James 5:11.

_____

_____

Let me take us to the end of the book of Job and recap. Scripture tells us that God made Job prosperous again and gave him twice as much as he had before (Job 42:10).

Family came to console and comfort him, and each one gave him silver and gold (verse 11). The Lord increased his livestock, gave him seven sons and three daughters (verses 12–13).

> After this, Job lived a hundred and forty years; he saw his children and their children to the fourth generation. And so he died, old and full of years. (Job 42:16–17)

Now we see part of what God brought about for Job. But I believe if we think that's all He did for Job, we've missed it. The most important thing "the Lord finally brought about" (James 5:11) is found in Philippians 3:10:

> I want to know Christ and the power of his resurrection and the fellowship of sharing in his sufferings, becoming like him in his death,

Knowing God, knowing Christ ... happens in our sufferings if we cling to hope in Him. We find when we are at the end of ourselves, He is all we need and He has been there all along.

Job came back to what he knew about his God and he fell to the ground in worship.

Paul, a New Testament believer, said in Philippians 3:10, "I want to know Christ."

> ... Paul already knew Christ as his Savior. But he wanted to know Him more intimately as his Lord. To know means "to know by experience" (gnonai). ...
>
> To experience the power of His resurrection was also the apostle's goal. The power which brought Christ forth from the dead now operates in believers' lives since they have been raised with Christ" (Col. 3:1). ...
>
> Paul also longed to share in the fellowship of Christ's sufferings and in so doing, to become like Him in His death. These sufferings were not Christ's substitutionary sufferings on the cross. Paul knew that those could not be shared. But he did desire to participate with Christ, since he was one of His, in suffering for the sake of righteousness.[3]

Just as He did for Paul, God ultimately "brought about" for Job a more intimate knowledge of knowing Him as Lord.

Write James 1:2–3.

_____

_____

... "mature and complete" with the knowledge of Jesus Christ (James 1:4).

Job's story is to teach and encourage us that through endurance in our suffering, we have hope.

It's amazing to me how God intends for me to walk through each lesson personally. This week I have been very attentive to listen to the Holy Spirit on the subject of suffering. He has opened my eyes to see those around me. Just two days ago in Sunday school, a woman was in tears because of her wayward son. Today in Bible study, a woman had to leave because of the intense pain she felt in her body. Every day this week, I have received calls at the church from people with critical financial needs. Everywhere we turn, on the other side of the world, in the US, within our state, our city, and our neighborhood, there is suffering. My friend Brenda has just returned from a mission trip to Haiti. She told me this morning on the phone about the poverty and the needs that she saw. Her heart is so broken. Suffering (sigh).

Tonight, it hit home for me when the phone rang, and I heard my daughter's voice on the other end shaken by a burden in her life. Trying my hardest to keep my voice steady and calm, though hurting inside for her, I reminded her that "God is still on the throne," reminding myself in the process.

A burdened heart of a mother no one can describe. Tonight, as I write, feeling concern for my child about what could be, I feel a kindred spirit toward our king's mother. I can relate to her loving her son with her whole heart and wanting nothing but a full life of health, happiness, and prosperity for her child—exactly what I want for mine. But, more than anything else, I want to see my children trusting the Lord as they follow Him all the days of their lives. That is by far most important to me. I believe it was for the king's mother also.

King Lemuel's mother needed the king to know that those who were perishing and in anguish could find relief through alcohol. But the king needed to remain sober.

Lord, I ask for Your strength, grace, mercy, and love to surround those who are suffering. Give me the words to encourage and direct them back to hope in You. And in my seasons of suffering, may I be reminded of the privilege to suffer for the sake of righteousness.

Give beer to those who are perishing, wine to those who are in anguish. (Proverbs 31:6)

Further Study:

The same man who wrote, "I want to know Christ and the power of his resurrection and the fellowship of sharing in his sufferings, becoming like him in his death," (Philippians 3:10) wrote from a heart who knew suffering.

The apostle Paul had been in prison, been flogged and had been exposed to death again and again.

From 2 Corinthians 11:24—28 fill in the missing words:
Five times I received from the Jews the _____ lashes minus one. Three times I was _____ _____, once I was _____ _____, three times I was _____, I spent a night and a day in the open sea. I have been constantly on the move. I have been in _____ from rivers, in danger from _____, in danger from my own countrymen, in _____ from Gentiles; in danger in the city, in _____ in the country, in danger at sea; and in danger from false brothers. I have _____ and _____ and have often gone without sleep; I have known _____, and thirst and have often gone without _____; I have been cold and naked. Besides everything else, I face daily the pressure of my _____ for all the _____.

Suffering. Who desires it? I don't. What I desire is to know my Savior as Lord and to know Him means to share in His suffering. In suffering, I feel His strength, grace, mercy, and love. In suffering, I become more compassionate toward others. In suffering, I share the heart of Christ.

Lemuel's mother said, "Son, help those who are perishing and those in anguish in their pain and suffering."

ENDNOTES:

[1]James Strong, *The New Strong's Expanded Exhaustive Concordance of the Bible Red-Letter Edition*, Dictionaries include contributions by John R. Kohlenberger, III (Nashville, TN: Thomas Nelson Publishers 2001)

[2]Salvatore P. Lucia, *Wine as Food and Medicine* (New York: The Blakiston Company, inc., 1954), https://babel.hathitrust.org/cgi/pt?id=mdp.39015065726229;view=1up;seq=8.

[3]*The Bible Knowledge Commentary*, eds. John F. Walvoord and Roy B. Zuck (Wheaton, IL: Victor Books, 1983)

Have Compassion, Son

PROVERBS 31:7

King Lemuel's mother's concern for others stemmed from a compassionate heart. She genuinely cared about the welfare of others. I want us to take time today to look at the contrast of alcohol for recreation and alcohol to dull pain and agony.

KJV	NASB	NIV
Let him drink, and forget his poverty, and remember his misery no more.	Let him drink and forget his poverty and remember his trouble no more.	Let them drink and forget their poverty and remember their misery no more.

The book of Esther would be a great example of alcohol for recreational use. After 180 days of displaying his vast wealth of his kingdom, King Xerxes gave a seven-day banquet. Wine was served, and by the king's command, each guest was allowed to drink in his own way, for the king instructed all the wine stewards to serve each man what he wished.

According to Esther 1:10, "On the seventh day ... King Xerxes was in high spirits from wine." I bet he was in high spirits after seven days! This kind of drinking was exactly what the king's mother feared for her son. I don't believe she was encouraging drinking excessively for anyone. I do think she knew people whom she had great compassion for because of their suffering. Maybe she could not relate personally, but the compassion she felt for them caused her heart to somehow understand why they did what they did.

Let them drink and forget their (his) poverty and remember their (his) misery (trouble) no more.

The word here for those who drink is linked to drunkards. Poverty means to be "poor"; And misery is "trouble, work, labor, toil."[1]

The queen mother wasn't condoning the drunkards' actions, but she had empathy for their emotional and mental distress. She understood how their distress might contribute to the choices they made in life.

I have seen the effects of too much alcohol in people close to me. The recreational use of it has caused me great pain in the past. Therefore, I used to be very judgmental toward anyone who drank, period. But over the past two years, I have gotten to know a recovering alcoholic. As I hear more of his story, I understand why he chose to turn to alcohol.

Was alcohol the right choice? No, of course not! But my compassion for him as he continues to share bits and pieces of his story overshadows the judgment that I once would have had for him.

My friend grew up in poverty. His parents were both alcoholics. He recalls often only having a piece of bread in his house to eat or nothing at all. When he was as young as six years old, he remembers his parents locking him out of the house while they binged on alcohol. He would often walk to his grandmother's house. She also lived in poverty. He told me that at his grandmother's he would sometimes go without sleep because he was afraid of the rats that he could hear scratching on the roof trying to get in. He struggled in school with learning disabilities, only getting a fifth-grade education at sixteen years old. As a young teen, he also chose alcohol and drugs as a way to cope with his difficult life. Eventually he became homeless. Living on the streets in a big city was all about survival, and his survival depended on his next drink.

The choices he made added to his misery. He drank to forget the misery. Yet after he sobered up, the anguish of the reality of his life was still there, so he drank again. And so the cycle continued.

I believe my friend was an example of the person King Lemuel's mother spoke of. Her heart chose compassion instead of judgment. She petitioned her son to realize that those hurting, perishing, and living in anguish were the ones who would benefit from alcohol, but it was not for him. His mind and heart had to remain pure so he could reign as such.

Compassion is defined as "sorrow for the sufferings or trouble of another, with the urge to help; pity; deep sympathy."[2]

Read Matthew 9:35–36.

Why did Jesus have compassion on the people?

_____

_____

Write Matthew 14:14.

_____

_____

Read Matthew 20:29–34; Luke 7:11–15.
How did Jesus respond in these two passages?

_____

_____

Read Hebrews 1:3 and write below.

_____

_____

Jesus told Philip when Philip asked to see the Father, "Anyone who has seen me has seen the Father " (John 14:9).

> You, O LORD, are a compassionate and gracious God, slow to anger, abounding in love and faithfulness. (Psalm 86:15)

The heart of God the Father and God the Son is a heart of compassion.

A sweet friend of mine has the gift of mercy. It amazes me the keen sense she has for the needs of others. She is so tender-hearted and makes herself available to meet their needs if at all possible. Compassion wells up inside her and pours out of her.

(Pause and sigh.) Then there's me. Without this gift of mercy, I have to totally depend on the Lord to pour that in me and coax it out of me. My heart isn't geared like my friend's. It's so easy for her. But, this is what I have realized. His heart is compassionate so mine can be also, but only when I allow His love and mercy to flow through me. This takes yielding to His Spirit in me.

Does compassion flow easily out of you or, like me, do you have to yield, allowing the Lord's compassionate heart to flow through you and out of you?

_____

_____

It has become a regular prayer request of mine that the Lord teach me His ways. I admire many people, but I can honestly say that I only want to be just like Jesus in every way. I am His through faith, and He is mine through His marvelous grace. Being His disciple is the greatest joy in my life. I am nothing without Him.

Allow the words of Dan Stolebarger, director of the Koinonia Institute, to take you back into history to Jesus' day to put discipleship in perspective. Discipleship should take on a whole new meaning for you.

> For Jews living in Jesus' day, there were three separate educational venues. The first was called *Bet Sefer*. At the ages of six through twelve, Jewish children began their formal education. Both boys and girls attended synagogue school and learned to read and write. The textbook was the Torah [the first five books of the Old Testament]

and the goal was not just to read but to memorize the sacred text....

Following this sacred milestone, usually the boy then began to learn the family trade. Only the best of the best continued on in their education. For the best of the best, the next educational opportunity was called *Bet Midrash*. Boys—from age 13 to 15—who were deemed worthy to continue their educational pursuits went on to study and memorize the entire Tanach [Old Testament], as well as learning the family trade. (It is noteworthy that few, if any, of Jesus disciples made it this far in their educational training.) Very few were selected for this pursuit.

Of those who finished *Bet Midrash*, again only the best of the best were able to pursue the final educational leg, which was called *Bet Talmud*. This was the longest in duration; it went from the age of 15 to 30. To participate, he must be invited by a Rabbi and, if selected, he would begin a process of grooming that would lead to the potential of becoming a Rabbi at age 30. Those who were chosen were referred to as *talmidim*. They would literally follow in the dust of their rabbi – desiring to emulate him in all of his mannerisms. They would eat the same food in exactly the same way as their rabbi. They would go to sleep and awake the same way as their rabbi and, more importantly, they would learn to study Torah and understand God the exact same way as their rabbi.

It appears that Jesus Himself followed this model. At twelve we know that He attended His first Passover in Jerusalem and He began His formal ministry at 30. The Bible is silent as far as His mentors, but we do know that He selected His disciples and, just like those young fifteen year olds when invited to *Bet Talmud*, they left everything to follow after this Rabbi from Galilee. No doubt they walked in His dust, wanting to be just like their Rabbi! They were His *Talmidim*! History and the Word reveal to us that Jesus trained His *talmidim* in three years (not fifteen) and His training was so inspired that they (His *talmidim*) literally changed the world![3]

Do you desire to be like the early followers of Jesus? Why or why not?

_____

_____

What words come to mind for what it takes to be a disciple of Jesus? I'll get you started.

Deliberate _____ _____

Committed _____ _____

_____ _____ _____

Pray right now asking God to help you follow after Rabbi Jesus, emulating Him in all of his mannerisms. May our testimonies be "I want to be just like Him."

Write Ezekiel 36:26–27.

_____

_____

A new heart and spirit is what a person receives when they surrender their life to the lordship of Jesus. **His Spirit in us leads us to be more like him.**

Finish Colossians 3:12.
As God's chosen people, holy and dearly loved, clothe yourselves with

_____

The queen mother's heart was that of compassion just like her God's. She chose compassion instead of judgment.

Lord, may I have a heart of compassion. It's not for me to judge others. You, O Lord are the only righteous judge.

_____

_____

Let them drink and forget their poverty and remember their misery no more. (Proverbs 31:7)

Further Study:

Read Mark 1:40–45.
What does this encounter that Jesus had with this man mean to you?

_____

_____

The man was disobedient to Jesus' command. What happened as a result?

_____

_____

> Because of the LORD's great mercy (love) we are
> not consumed, for his compassions never fail.
> (Lamentations 3:22)

The queen said, "Son, rule your kingdom with compassion because the Lord your God is a compassionate God!"

ENDNOTES:

[1]James Strong, *The Strongest Strong's Exhaustive Concordance of the Bible*, eds. John R. Kohlenberger and James A. Swanson (Grand Rapids, MI: Zondervan, 2001).

[2]*Webster's New World Dictionary of the American Language*, Concise Ed., s.v. "compassion."

[3]Dan Stolebarger, "Discipleship vs. Talmidim," Koinonia House, http://www.khouse.org/articles/2005/616.

Speak Up for Others

PROVERBS 31:8

Recently a guest speaker came to our church to share about the work he does helping abused children. There was no doubt about the love he had for the ones God had brought his way. His face lit up when he spoke of lives changed through his organization. They are speaking up for the children who can't speak for themselves.

KJV	NASB	NIV
Open thy mouth for the dumb in the cause of all such as are appointed to destruction.	Open your mouth for the mute, for the rights of all the unfortunate.	Speak up for those who cannot speak for themselves, for the rights of all who are destitute.

As I listened, I was so thankful for the calling on his life. He and others continue to meet the physical, mental, and psychological needs of so many young people. It didn't take long to see that the love he has for children was because of the love he has for Christ. As he shared about the decisions made for Jesus just in the past year alone it was evident the mission of his calling was to introduce the kids to Love.

At the end of the service, our congregation shared Holy Communion together. As I tightly gripped the little cracker in my hand, I asked the Lord, "Why did You give Your body for me?" A few minutes later, as I held the little cup of juice, this time with tears standing in my eyes, I asked, "Why did You spill Your blood for me?" In the depth of my soul, His still, small voice responded, "Because of love."

I firmly believe this lesson may be the most important word we will receive from God. The subject is love. I can think of nothing more important than love.

Read Luke 7:36–50 and answer the questions.

Why was Jesus in this house?

_____

What occurred after dinner?

_____

_____

What type of woman does Luke 7:37 say she was?

_____

Write Luke 7:38.

_____

_____

Jesus said to Simon in verse 47: "Her many sins have been forgiven—for she loved much."

Why do you think her heart was so tender toward Jesus?

_____

_____

Luke does not identify this woman by name. According to *Who's Who In the Bible*, "The tradition of the Church has from early times identified Mary of Magdala with the woman living an immoral life in the city."[1]

As you recall, Mary of Bethany, sister of Martha and Lazarus also showed him gratitude by anointing Jesus' feet with a pint of pure nard, an expensive perfume (John 12:3).

From Luke 7:36–50 list what Mary did in honoring Jesus.

_____

_____

What was Jesus' response?

_____

Speak up (open your mouth) for those who cannot speak for themselves,

What reasons would Mary have for not being able to speak up for herself?

_____

_____

She was a woman and a sinful one at that. She was also a guest in someone's home. It is apparent that her focus was on Jesus, but I believe she must have been aware that she was being scrutinized among those present. Any one of these reasons along with any of yours would have given her cause not to speak up for herself.

for the rights of all who are destitute (unfortunate).
Now read Mark 12:41–44 and Luke 21:1–4.

What did this widow do?

_____

_____

What was the heart condition of both Mary and this widow?

_____

_____

Jesus took notice of both women and stood up for them. Through His loving kindness, Jesus spoke up for these women and honored them. Think about this. Jesus recognized Mary and the poor widow's acts of service because their service was evidence of their heart condition. Both women were deliberate from the overflow of their grateful hearts toward God who, in Mary's case, delivered her, and in the poor widow's case, would deliver her and supply all her needs. I have to let out a sigh right now and say, "It's about relationship." His loving kindness had drawn them into the relationship they had with Him. They knew Him as Creator, Savior, and Sustainer, and they trusted Him enough to offer what they had. Their acts of service were nothing less than worship because they focused on Him and gave from their gratitude. And He noticed.

King Lemuel's mother was led to teach her son about this same loving kindness. The king had the power to defend those who could not defend themselves.

Look up Proverbs 3:27 and write it below.

_____

_____

Our ability to give "good" to others is loving kindness. Loving kindness in the original Hebrew language means "unfailing love, loyal love, devotion." [2] In all twenty-six times that "loving kindness" appears in the King James Version, it is referring to the Lord. It's only through His loving kindness that we are able to "not withhold good from those who deserve it."

Jesus said of Mary, "for she loved much." In these last days before the return of Jesus, we have certainly become a "me society." It seems the world has become very good at loving itself. The problem with that is when you only love yourself, you fail to love God and others. Christian sibling! We are a new creation in Christ. We are different! If you have gotten caught up in the world's view, it's time for God to draw you back to your first love,

Him. It's "because of love" that He longs to teach us about who He is.

> If anyone acknowledges that Jesus is the Son of God, God lives in him and he in God. And so we know and rely on the love God has for us. God is love. Whoever lives in love lives in God, and God in him. (1 John 4:15–16)

In Proverbs 31, God is showing us this in His Word about Lemuel's mother—"for she loved much." She knew her God as Love. Because she relied on the love of God, she taught her son to speak up for those who could not speak up for themselves, showing them the loving kindness of God. This only happens with God in us.

Jesus had some unfinished business to take care of after His resurrection. He had spoken on the subject of love so often in the past, but one particular morning He would speak of love from a new angle.

Jesus stood on the shore early that morning by the Sea of Tiberias. Peter and some of the disciples had taken the boat out the night before to fish. Peter certainly knew about fishing; he was after all, an expert—a fisherman by trade. I'm sure they had lots of good ole fish tales, probably even embellished ones like my papa and I use to tell when I was a child. But this time the well seemed dry, and not just from the lack of fish.

Their friend, their Rabbi, their Savior whom they loved was no longer with them in the boat. What if a storm came up and they became fearful? Who would calm it and speak to them about faith? He had already appeared to them two times since

His resurrection. But so much had happened in the past days; so much they wanted to understand but certainly couldn't comprehend it all.

Although John outran Peter to the tomb after hearing the report of Jesus' missing body, Peter was the one who brushed by John and entered to see for himself. Peter loved Jesus with all his heart. He had even cut off the right ear of Malchus at His arrest. Yes, Peter's behavior had been rash and harsh. His method to action was not what Jesus desired, so he was rebuked, yet, I believe Peter's motivation was from a heart brimming over with love for Jesus. Peter had made lots of mistakes, especially when he denied even knowing Jesus, not once, twice, but three times. So much to take in, the last days, months, years, but even now, as Jesus stood on that shore watching them, He continued to bless them.

> He called out to them, "Friends, haven't you any fish?" "No," they answered. He said, "Throw your net on the right side of the boat and you will find some." When they did, they were unable to haul the net because of the large number of fish. Then the disciple whom Jesus loved said to Peter, "It is the Lord!!" (John 21:5-7)

Impulsive Peter couldn't wait to get to Him, so he jumped out of the boat. Talk about deliberate! We can certainly take a huge lesson from Peter. He jumped into the waters so that he could once again be by his Master's side. The fishing boat obviously couldn't get him there fast enough for his liking.

Listen dear sibling, when we wake to the first light of day with the overwhelming desire in our hearts to be close to His side, it's like we see Jesus on the shore. As we go directly to Him in prayer and the study of His Word where He speaks to us, we have jumped into the waters, swimming with all our might to get to Him. We will be blessed by His presence. His early disciples were, and we will be too!

The disciples arrived on shore to a warm campfire and sweet fellowship. Jesus fed the hungry men both physically and spiritually.

> When they had finished eating, Jesus said to Simon Peter, "Simon son of John, do you truly love me more than these?" (John 21:15)

The word for love here is *agape*, God-size love, the highest form of love.

Peter's response: "Yes, Lord," he said, "you know that I love you." (John 22:15)

Good answer, Peter—except the Greek word used here is *phileo*, which means "to love, to have affection and regard of a very high order."

Jesus moved on to Peter's mission.

[He] said: "Feed my lambs." (John 21:15)

In other words, "Take care in teaching my people."

Again Jesus said, "Simon, son of John, do you truly love me?" (John 21:16)

The Greek word used by Jesus once again for love was *agape*.

Peter's response describing his love for Jesus was *phileo*.

"Yes, Lord, you know that I love you." (John 21:16)

Reaffirming Peter's mission, Jesus said, "Take care of my sheep." (John 21:16)

A third time Jesus asked the same question of Peter, with one difference. He used the word *phileo* instead of *agape*. Jesus' *agape* had not changed. It's almost as though Jesus was asking, "Do you love me, Peter, like I love you?" Peter loved Jesus with the love capacity that he had. Jesus already knew that Peter could only *phileo* Him, but Jesus wanted Peter to know that He loved Peter with the highest love. This love Peter didn't quite understand, but he would and he did. Peter certainly would have to establish his love for Jesus to carry out the mission of caring and feeding His sheep. But, more importantly than that, Peter would have to carry the love that Jesus had for him to withstand persecution and death on a cross.

Right now in my mind I am recalling story after story in the gospels that project the *agape* of Jesus. But there's one that stands out like no other. Go with me to John 13 and allow me to set the scene for you:

It was just before the Passover Feast. The time had come for Jesus to finish His part of the salvation plan for the world. He would be going to the Father soon. His time was limited. He had more to show and tell His disciples. He would be leaving them to carry on the mission of telling the world about a Savior, the Messiah ... about Himself. They would have to understand not only about His love for them but also His love for an unsaved world.

Having loved his own who were in the world,
he now showed them the full extent of his love.
(John 13:1)

This act of *agape* involved a foot washing ceremony.

[Jesus, as servant] got up from the meal, took off
his outer clothing, and wrapped a towel around
his waist. After that, he poured water into a basin
and began to wash his disciples' feet, drying
them with the towel that was wrapped around
him. (John 13:4–5)

Jesus needed His disciples to know about *agape*, which would include serving others. As Christians, the process of knowing God better leads to loving Him more. As we depend upon Him, our love capacity for Him and others will expand in us. As we allow His love to consume us, it fills us, swelling our hearts to a new size. Don't miss this! It's His *agape* in us that replaces our *phileo* in our hearts. His dimension of love is infinite. Our service to others is the test of how we have allowed God's love to swell our hearts to a bigger size. If His love capacity is infinite, then ours can be too!

After a time of conversation passed, The Bible tells us that:

Jesus was troubled in spirit and testified, "I tell
you the truth, one of you is going to betray me."
His disciples stared at one another, at a loss to
know which of them he meant. One of them, the
disciple whom Jesus loved, was reclining next to
him. Simon Peter motioned to this disciple and
said, "Ask him which one he means." Leaning

back against Jesus, he asked him, "Lord, who is it?" (John 13:21–25)

This is so rich! Jesus' act of love included all the disciples. He washed each of their feet. Yet, one of them, Judas, was about to betray Him. Of course, Jesus already knew about this betrayal long before He revealed it to His disciples. Here's my point that you can't miss. Jesus treated each of the disciples the same. The disciples didn't have a clue who He was talking about. There was absolutely no difference in His love for the betrayer and His love for the other disciples. Judas' future action against Jesus had nothing to do with His love for Judas. What kind of love is this? It's God-size love!

The queen mother knew that her son had the power to fight for those entrusted to him. The power that he possessed because he belonged to God was, in fact, God's. She knew that he needed to be obedient to his calling. She also knew that God would be faithful in helping him as he reached out and helped others. As the king drew from the love of God, his acts of service toward others would, like Mary and the poor widow, be nothing less than undefiled worship.

King Lemuel's mother instructed her son from a heart who knew Love. Through His love, her heart was bent toward showing others kindness, speaking up for those who could not speak for themselves.

Lord, give me the courage to speak up for others. Your loving kindness and Your agape love flowing through me will empower me and will be my guide.

Speak up for those who cannot speak for themselves, for the rights of all who are destitute. (Proverbs 31:8)

Further Study:

Write Matthew 22:37–39.

This passage sums up the teachings (law) of God.

Read 1 Corinthians 13:1–8.
The word for love here is agape.

(*Agape*) love rejoices with the truth. It always protects, always trusts, always hopes, always perseveres. (*Agape*) love never fails.

Now go back and read this passage once more, but out loud this time. Replace the word God for every instance of love because "God is love" (1 John 4:8). I'll get you started. God is patience, God is kind. God does not envy ...

Thank you for your hard work. Keep studying. God is doing a work in you.

ENDNOTES:
[1]Joan Comay and Ronald Brownrigg, *Who's Who In The Bible*, (Avenel,New Jersey: Wing Books 1980).
[2]*Nelson's New Illustrated Bible Dictionary*, ed. Ronald F. Young-blood (Nashville: Thomas Nelson,1995).

Judge Fairly & Defend Others

PROVERBS 31:9

Our days consist of a series of judgment calls. We make judgments for ourselves as well as others. To judge means to decide, lead, or defend. Our decisions and how we lead and defend throughout the day can certainly reflect wisdom, discernment, and knowledge. As believers and followers of Jesus Christ, that is our goal. But we so often fall short, don't we? I often make decisions with a bad attitude, critical spirit, and sometimes with a sassy mouth. Oh, my husband would have to say AMEN to that one! What about you? Can you relate? As we judge, the question that we have to ask ourselves is how we are judging.

KJV	NASB	NIV
Open thy mouth, judge righteously, and plead the cause of the poor and needy.	Open your mouth, judge righteously, and defend the rights of the afflicted and needy.	Speak up and judge fairly; defend the rights of the poor and needy.

It's confession time. Just a few days ago I had something happen that irritated me to no end, and I shared it. And I shared it more than once. I felt mistreated and angry about someone's actions that caused me extra work. Then it happened. I did the same thing to someone else. Really? Seriously. Of course, I justified it in my mind that it was okay, but God opened my eyes and basically said, "Wait a minute..." It was one of those times when something is revealed to you and you just can't speak. All you can do is just sit there stunned and convicted. Jesus said:

> "Do not judge, and you will not be judged. Do not condemn, and you will not be condemned. Forgive, and you will be forgiven. Give, and it will be given to you. A good measure, pressed down, shaken together and running over, will be poured into your lap. For with the measure you use, it will be measured to you." (Luke 6:37-38)

When Jesus said, "Do not judge." What type of judging was He referring to?

Jesus goes on to say:

> "Why do you look at the speck of sawdust in your brother's eye and pay no attention to the plank in your own eye? How can you say to your brother, 'Brother, let me take the speck out of your eye,' when you yourself fail to see the plank in your own eye? You hypocrite, first take the plank out of your eye, and then you will see clearly to remove the speck from your brother's eye." (Luke 6:41-42)

Many of us shoot our mouths off about other people's actions, but we fail to see that we are also guilty of the same thing. Honestly, we wear such blinders! Nobody else can live up to our perfection. O Holy God, help us! What Pharisees we are! I don't know about you, but some days I feel like I need to wear duct tape over my mouth. There have been times in the church office that I need not speak at all. I have even put my lips together and used the hand motion of taping my mouth shut to my pastor so that I will think about my words before they exit my mouth.

Speak up (open thy mouth) and judge fairly (righteously),

Let's review so we can put it all together. In the KJV it uses the phrasing "open thy mouth."

This comes from the Hebrew word for "open wide." The word judge means "to decide, lead, defend, execute a judgment." And righteously means "rightness, acting in accordance to a proper (God's) standard."[1]

King Lemuel's mother is telling her son here, "Open your mouth wide (be deliberate) and decide, defend, and lead according to the standard God has put before you, Son."

Remember, the king would have gone back to the Torah (Genesis, Exodus, Leviticus, Numbers, and Deuteronomy), God's teachings, His instruction on how to live life. You and I have the fulfillment of those teachings in Jesus Christ. We look to Him for the example.

King Lemuel had the responsibility as king to make decisions every day concerning others. He would have to make judgment calls concerning those entrusted under his leadership. The queen mother wanted him to realize this was a sacred assignment and should not be taken lightly.

Now, what about you and me? We may not be a king or queen, but we, too, make judgments every day. Let's be real and personal for just a minute. Let's take off the Christian masks of what we are supposed to be and get real.

How many times a day do you judge others? If it helps, ask yourself this way: How often do I make decisions, lead, or defend others throughout the day? (Circle your answer below.)

All day long   Often   Little   Not at all

In this judging of others, is it a righteous judging? Be honest and explain your answer.

The queen was addressing her son to help him remember who he belonged to. He was the son of the Father of mercy and grace, and he was to mimic those actions.

According to *Nelson's New Illustrated Bible Dictionary*, mercy is "the aspect of God's love that causes Him to help the miserable, just as grace is the aspect of His love that moves him to forgive the guilty."[2]

So I have to ask myself the hard questions. How am I judging others? In other words: How am I deciding, leading, and defending others? Am I merciful as I deal with others? Am I accusing if they are less than perfect? Am I critical toward them in my thoughts if they make decisions that I wouldn't necessarily make? Sad to admit, but I often am.

Look back at Luke 6:37–38 and verses 41–42. Read them again, out loud this time, and allow the words to penetrate your heart.

What conviction do you feel from these passages?

_____

_____

The next part of this instruction from the king's mother is a natural progression of godly counsel. First, we have to know the standard that God has set, then with that, move to:

plead the cause (defend the rights) of the poor and needy.

How easy is it for you to plead the cause for others?

_____

_____

What motivates you to do so?

_____

_____

It certainly takes surrender of self to judge others righteously and to plead the cause of the poor and needy. It may even be easier to stand up for those less fortunate than to judge righteously.

In the NIV translation of our verse today, there's a semicolon between the two thoughts. Look at the KJV and NASB, and fill in the blank.

Open (thy) your mouth, judge righteously, _____ plead (defend) the cause (rights) of the poor (afflicted) and needy.

The queen is saying first things first. Judge others righteously, then use that same standard to plead the cause of the poor and needy.

Several years ago, while driving down our country road, the sun revealed the condition of my glasses—dirty. I stopped my car in the middle of the road to clean them. As I was putting them back on my face, the Holy Spirit impressed these words upon me: "Ask Me for spiritual eyes to see." So I asked Him for eyes to see what He sees. Not long after that, I was worshipping God in my living room, and He dropped an image into my mind. Actually, it was more like a video playing.

I was looking in on an operating room. Trained professionals were all around monitoring and looking over a body on a gurney. A doctor was working on the innermost parts of the heart. Those around him were amazed at his exact expertise and precision. It was so obvious that he was targeting diseased areas from the reactions in the room. The body on that gurney was my own. The Lord revealed to me that my heart was laid open, exposed, but He, the Great Physician, was working to correct the sicknesses of my heart, spiritually.

At the time this all took place, I was experiencing problems with my physical heart. So as I recall this time, I can tell you that God brought it all together for me. You see, I had been praying so much for my physical heart, but God wanted me to know that more serious symptoms were associated with my spiritual heart. He allowed me to see what He was doing by giving me spiritual eyes to see. Has God given you spiritual eyes to see your exposed heart lately? What did you see?

_____

_____

God continues to show me the spiritually diseased parts of my heart and also the weak parts that could lead to potential disease later. He's over me performing surgery. It's call sanctification. If you are His, He's working on you also. He's faithful to it! The one thing I'm sure of is when the Great Physician has the knife, deep cuts are made, true character is revealed, and complete healing takes place.

As God faithfully reveals to me my spiritual condition, He is showing me about His great mercy.

> He does not treat us as our sins deserve or repay us according to our iniquities. For as high as the heavens are above the earth, so great is his love for those who fear him; as far as the east is from the west, so far has he removed our transgressions from us. As a father has compassion on his children, so the LORD has compassion on those who fear him; for he knows how we are formed, he remembers that we are dust. (Psalm 103:10–14)

God also reminds me on a regular basis of Philippians 2:14:

Do everything without complaining or arguing.

God has given us a command and we are failing royally on a daily basis. Most days, complaining and arguing is all we do. God commands our surrender. He does! It's the only way. We can't hold on to what we want and how we feel. Our desires must become what He desires for us. Dear sibling, this is truth. Surrender of self gives way to a clearer picture of Jesus in us.

Read Luke 9:18-20 in your Bible.

Although Jesus questioned the disciples on what others were saying about who He was, the most important thing to Jesus at that moment was who the disciples knew Him to be. He asked the questions so that they could talk through not only what they had heard, but, most importantly, what they believed to be true. Asking questions was not unusual for rabbis. They asked questions to see how much their disciples understood. The rabbis needed to know what their disciples knew so they would know where to pick up with their teaching.

Jesus was human, so as a rabbi, He would naturally ask the questions. But Jesus was also completely God. He already knew the answers to His questions. Jesus already knew who they knew Him to be. He needed them to search their hearts and speak it out loud to confirm the truth.

As all of us in our spiritual journeys, Peter had quite the bumpy road ahead of him. Praise God that he was clueless as to the plans before him, or he might have turned and ran as fast as his legs would allow.

Since we have Peter's future laid out before us in Holy Scripture, we can praise God as we realize that the "Rock" who would build God's church spoke first. How appropriate!!

Peter answered, "The Christ of God" [the Promised Messiah]. (Luke 9:20)

Jesus was speaking to all of His disciples; yet Peter was the one who spoke up. Maybe Jesus' eyes turned to His natural-born leader for the response or maybe Jesus' natural-born leader spoke first because of the power of the conviction in his heart.

Jesus strictly warned them not to tell this to anyone. (Luke 9:21)

Now read Luke 9:22–25.

Write verse 23 below.
Then he said to them all:

_____

_____

Look at Matthew's account at 16:13–21.

> Peter took Him aside and began to rebuke him,
> "Never, Lord!" he said. "This shall never happen
> to you!" Jesus turned and said to Peter, "Get be-
> hind me, Satan! You are a stumbling block to me;
> you do not have in mind the things of God, but
> the things of men." Then Jesus said to his

disciples, "If anyone would come after me, he must deny himself and take up his cross and follow me." (Matthew 16:22–24)

Dear sibling, we are to put aside selfish ambition of pride and earthly desires so that we can shoulder our cross of love, forgiveness, sacrifice ... and run after God with all we've got. This is an act of deliberateness in following Him.

Jesus spoke of the sacrifices that lay ahead for His disciples. Salvation is free, but discipleship costs everything. Yet only the self-sacrificing disciple will truly "find" his or her life.

We need change to come about in us which requires surrender. You and I can't and won't become more like Jesus without it.

Create in me a pure heart, O God and renew a steadfast spirit within me. (Psalm 51:10)

David wrote this after he sinned against God with Bathsheba. His heart was exposed, and he saw the need for a pure heart. David knew that a clean heart would require change, and to have what it would take to endure change, he would need a steadfast spirit. Why? Because the change of heart requires time, and time requires patience and endurance. We need a steadfast spirit so that we can run the race, for "perseverance must finish its work so that you may be mature and complete, not lacking anything" (James 1:4).

Several years ago, Walt Disney came out with a movie called The Princess Diaries. Remember it? Mia, a fifteen-year-old, unpopular, clumsy, diamond-in-the-rough girl, struggles to fit in.

She finds out that she is next in line for the throne of Genovia. She is royalty.

Mia's grandmother, the queen of Genovia, comes to town to see the granddaughter she has never met. Mia agrees to go through princess lessons, which include an appearance transformation. The princess lessons would also teach her how to eat, sit, speak, dance, and wave like a princess.

Mia gets a reality check fairly quickly on how the title of princess will change her life. She feels unworthy and untalented. My favorite line in the movie is when Joe, head security man, says to Mia, "Nobody can quit being who they are!"

As a daughter of the King, we have princess status. Sometimes we refuse to go through the princess lessons, don't we? Just like Mia, we want to give up. But, fellow traveler, we will go through the lessons one way or another. God has put me through difficult classes that I have failed miserably. I have had to retake more life courses than I care to recall. Being a princess has responsibilities we are not up for. Looking in on our ordinary life looks less challenging, so we stick with what's easy. But we are not ordinary— we are extraordinary!

Surrendering daily is difficult, but it is necessary. Jesus tells us that surrender is the only way to experience discipleship.

King Lemuel's mother was a disciple. She knew that surrender required putting aside selfish ambitions. Her focus was on God, and she was deeply committed in teaching her son the ways of righteous living.

> **Speak up and judge fairly; defend the rights of the poor and needy. (Proverbs 31:9)**

Test Yourself:

Read 1 Corinthians 10:31 and answer the following questions:

Are the things I am saying bringing glory to God?

Are the things I am doing bringing glory to God?

Pray according to your answers above.

_____

_____

_____

_____

ENDNOTES:

[1] James Strong, *The Strongest Strong's Exhaustive Concordance of the Bible*, eds. John R. Kohlenberger and James A. Swanson (Grand Rapids, MI: Zondervan, 2001).

[2] *Nelson's New Illustrated Bible Dictionary*, ed. Ronald F. Young-blood (Nashville: Thomas Nelson, 1995).

Part 2

ADVICE FROM THE KING'S MOTHER

TO HER SON ON WHAT KIND OF

WIFE HE SHOULD CHOOSE

Interlude

We now will transition from the instruction King Lemuel's mother gave her son about how he should rule as king to what he should desire in a wife.

Allow me a short break before the next lesson to thank you for your perseverance. I am praying for you once again as I write. In seeking the Holy Spirit's guidance for what I should pray, He brought someone to mind: my twelve-year-old niece Laine. Laine has always had a heart for missions (so does her little brother, Ben). I can recall some birthdays when Laine and Ben asked their parents if their parties could be a time of giving back to a ministry.

Laine loves animals and has volunteered at their local humane society on a regular basis for a couple of years. On her tenth birthday, her friends were asked to bring gifts for her furry friends. That year gifts of dog and cat food, collars, blankets, etc. were all donated to her favorite charity. I recall my sister, Krystal telling me that Laine was trying to explain how she felt about her volunteer work one day. Krystal patiently waited as Laine put into words what her ten-year-old heart felt. Finally, she said, "My heart is full."

I am asking God that your heart might be found full to the point of overflowing because of His love and plan for you as He continues to mold and shape you into the woman He created you to be.

I believe that King Lemuel's mother might have said "My heart is full," because she was in relationship with the One who filled it. She instructed her son because of the knowledge and wisdom she herself possessed. The words from her mouth were from a heart that lived out her instruction because her lifestyle was a reflection of the words she spoke. We can start with her as our example to see what is considered a Proverbs 31 woman.

Let's review before we continue on. Add whatever might have been revealed to you.

- Lemuel's mother spoke words of instruction to her son from a burdened heart because of the vows she had made to the Lord.
- She warned him against women and alcohol, which could ruin him, and directed him toward doing the will of God.
- From a compassionate heart, Lemuel's mother reminded her son that through obedience to the law of God, people would be taken care of.
- In boldness and confidence she told her son to be brave and speak up for those who couldn't speak for themselves.

_____

_____

Is She Virtuous?

PROVERBS 31:10

Beginning with verse 10 through verse 31, we find one of the alphabetical acrostic poems in the Bible. Each verse begins with a different letter of the Hebrew alphabet in the proper order. This poem of the biblical virtuous woman is designed to show the kind of wife women should emulate and the kind of wife men should choose.

KJV	NASB	NIV
Who can find a virtuous woman? For her price is far above rubies.	An excellent wife, who can find? For her worth is far above jewels.	A wife of noble character who can find? She is worth far more than rubies.

Lemuel's mother outlined the model for a virtuous (noble, excellent) woman (wife). She is clearly a woman of position and ability. And just so we understand, she is not easy to find.

In your experience and personal opinion, why is a virtuous woman hard to find?

_____

_____

Read Ecclesiastes 7:23–28. What did King Solomon find?

_____

_____

Our society certainly does not encourage a woman to be upright. Society today encourages a worldly view that includes folly and wickedness. I wonder what kind of wife King Solomon would find today if he lived in this day and age. I would hope that his search wouldn't be disappointing since I know virtuous women. I guess it would depend on where his search took him.

This word "virtuous" (or noble) in Hebrew is *hayil*.[1] It means valor. This term was often used to denote strong men going into battle. This word describes Gideon in Judges 6:12 and Naaman in 2 Kings 5:1.

> When the angel of the LORD appeared to Gideon, he said, "The LORD is with you, mighty warrior." (Judges 6:12)

> Now Naaman was commander of the army of the king of Aram. He was a great man in the sight of his master and highly regarded, because through

him the L ORD had given victory to Aram. He was
a valiant soldier, but he had leprosy. (2 Kings
5:1)

Man (or woman) of valor = mighty warrior.

This word *hayil* is also the word that appears in Proverbs 31:10
for virtuous, noble, or excellent, depending on the translation.
The American Heritage Dictionary defines valor as "strong, courage, fearlessness."[2] We will see throughout this section that our
Proverbs 31 woman is a woman of strength, courage, and fearlessness. *Hayil* implies one who conquers adversity. A woman of
hayil (valor) is, therefore, one who triumphs over the difficulties
of life.

Write Proverbs 12:4.

In Genesis 2:18, "the L ORD God said, 'It is not good for the
man to be alone. I will make a helper suitable for him.'" After
God made the animals and Adam named them, Scripture la-
ments, "But for Adam no suitable helper was found" (Genesis
2:20). So God created Eve to be a suitable helpmate for Adam.

Keeping this in mind, and also the meaning of *hayil*, in what ways is a virtuous (noble, excellent) woman her husband's crown?

_____

_____

Where do you think her strength, courage, and fearlessness come from? Hint: your answer is found in Proverbs 31:30.

_____

_____

We will look at verse 30 closer in a future lesson, but since this verse describes how a woman becomes virtuous, we will take a peek now. I want to focus on "a woman who fears the Lord." You see, we are not born virtuous. It's not even something that happens as we get older and, hopefully, wiser. Remember, a virtuous woman is hard to find. Please hear this. You and I can only become virtuous through our relationship with the Lord. With our commitment to be obedient depending solely on Him, He makes us virtuous.

Jesus said when calling His disciples, Peter and Andrew, "Come, follow me ... and I will **make** you fishers of men" (Matthew 4:19).

This morning on my way to work, I was praying about someone I am trying very hard to tolerate. I literally have to clench my mouth shut while my mind is filtering through the words that are about to exit when I am with this person. My desire is to always be kind. I realize that once my words are spoken, I can't take them back. As I was talking to the Lord about this, He reminded me of this verse in Matthew 4:19. It confirms to me His faithfulness to mold and, yes, chip off the rough edges of my character so that I will become more and more like Jesus. He knows how badly I want to live my life in total obedience to Him. I am not only His child, but I am also His disciple. I am always learning from Him through His Word. I pray that my life reflects an effort to live in the fear of the Lord.

What does it mean to "fear the Lord"?

_____

_____

In your answer, you might have used words like awesome, awe, great, praise, exalt, honor, reverence, and worship.

"To fear the Lord" (sigh) ... turn to Psalm 145:3 in your Bible.

One of my favorite times is when the house is quiet and I'm curled up in my favorite spot on our sofa reading my favorite book, my Bible. What makes it even better is when God causes a verse or a passage to jump off the page at me. I love to highlight in my Bible, so it's during these times when I know God is using those holy highlighters only found in the heavenly places to wow me!

This verse, Psalm 145:3, has been holy highlighted the past few days as I have pondered on what it means to "fear the Lord."

> Great is the LORD and most worthy of praise; his greatness no one can fathom. (Psalm 145:3)

Read this verse out loud and meditate on it. Let it soak in every crevice of your mind and heart.

What is one way God has recently shown you "his greatness no one can fathom" in a personal way?

When you reflect on that example in your own life, does it cause you to praise Him and exalt Him as God of the universe? Maybe when you think about His greatness you want to sing a song to Him. Or maybe you are speechless, and all you can do is fall facedown before Him.

What is your response to His greatness?

Last night in our Wednesday night Bible study, our pastor said that sometimes he feels the presence of the Lord so strongly in our Worship Center that he feels he can only get to the pulpit by crawling there or that he is unable to go at all because he feels so unworthy.

So enters the "fear of the Lord," and this, my friend, is the heart of the Proverbs 31 woman. Look at her, this woman of valor, and realize her worth. She is a woman of great value to her God and those around her. Oh, yes! She is most definitely rarer and more precious than the most valued stones.

A wife of noble character who can find? She is worth far more than rubies. (Proverbs 31:10)

Wrap Up: A virtuous (noble, excellent, woman of valor—*hayil* in Hebrew) woman is a mighty warrior of God. She is a woman of strength, courage, and fearlessness. A woman of valor (*hayil*) triumphs over the difficulties of life because she is a woman who fears the Lord. Through her relationship with Him, He makes her who she is, a woman of great value to Him and others.

Respond to your God in the space below.

_____

_____

_____

_____

Endnotes:

[1]James Strong, *The Strongest Strong's Exhaustive Concordance of the Bible*, eds. John R. Kohlenberger and James A. Swanson (Grand Rapids, MI: Zondervan, 2001).
[2]*The American Heritage Dictionary*, Second College Edition, s.v. "valor."

She Is Trustworthy

PROVERBS 31:11

Lemuel's mother instructed her son to look for a virtuous woman even though she would be hard to find. In the verses to follow, we will see what attributes the virtuous woman possesses.

The first attribute we will explore is that the virtuous woman is trustworthy.

KJV	NASB	NIV
The heart of her husband doth safely trust in her, so that he shall have no need of spoil.	The heart of her husband trusts in her, and he will have no lack of gain.	Her husband has full confidence in her and lacks nothing of value.

In the last lesson we referred back to Gideon, the mighty warrior, and Naaman, the valiant soldier, as men of valor (*hayil*) who were virtuous. God has also given us a virtuous woman in Scripture: a woman named Ruth. Know her? The book that is named after this virtuous woman comes after Judges in your Bible. The events of Ruth took place during the time in Israel's history when the judges ruled.

Finish writing Ruth 3:11: All my fellow townsmen know that you [Ruth] are a woman of _____ _____ [virtuous].

Allow me to review or introduce you to Ruth (Ruth 1:1–14):

A family from Bethlehem, Elimelech, Naomi, his wife, and their two sons, Mahlon and Kilion, moved to Moab to escape a famine in Bethlehem.

According to *The Path* blog, "ancient Moab (now Jordan) was a mountainous strip running along the eastern shore of the Dead Sea and the southern section of the Jordan River."[1] Their journey to Moab would have been about forty to sixty miles, depending on the path chosen. "Both the Israelites and Moabites spoke Hebrew and shared many of the same customs, but biblical history records that they were often in conflict, a sort of "on-again, off-again" relationship."[2]

While in Moab, Mahlon and Kilion took wives, Ruth and Orpah. Within a few years, Elimelech, Mahlon, and Kilion all died, leaving Naomi and her daughter-in-laws widowed.

Scripture says that Naomi heard how God was providing food for His people, so she decided to go back home. She urged Ruth and Orpah to stay in Moab with their people and their gods. After an emotional scene, Orpah made the decision to stay in Moab, but Ruth left everything she had ever known to go with Naomi to Bethlehem.

So here she is, Ruth, center stage—our virtuous woman, a woman who feared the Lord. Ruth was trustworthy. She trusted the Lord, yes, but He also trusted her so much that He Himself put her in the position to directly impact those around her and future generations to come, which we will see over the next few weeks.

We will be looking in on Ruth from time to time through-out the rest of this study. I promise you will know this virtuous woman well by the end of our time together.

What do you think it takes for a husband, family member, or friend to have full confidence in someone?

_____

_____

Before moving on, let's look at some definitions:

Trust: confidence in the integrity, ability, character, and truth of a person or thing.[3]

Trustworthy: warranting trust; reliable.[4]

Think of someone you know who you consider trustworthy. What makes you trust him or her?

_____

_____

The person that immediately comes to my mind has these attributes. She is a good listener. She earnestly cares. She gives godly counsel, and she does not gossip.

Consider the following Scripture verses:

> When words are many, sin is not absent, but he who holds his tongue is wise. (Proverbs 10:19)

> Dear children, let us not love with words or tongue but with actions and in truth. (1 John 3:18)

> Perfume and incense bring joy to the heart, and the pleasantness of one's friend springs from his earnest counsel. (Proverbs 27:9)

> A gossip betrays a confidence, but a trustworthy man keeps a secret. (Proverbs 11:13)

Are you a trustworthy person? Explain your answer.

Would those closest to you (spouse, children, parents, friends, or coworkers) say they can trust you? Why or why not?

For several years I was in management with a couple of different companies. Many times I had to make hard decisions that I thought was in the company's best interest. Those decisions most always affected people. I never wanted to make decisions, especially the tough ones, carelessly. I prayed and, yes, often stressed about them. I recall one such time like it was yesterday. I painfully had to dismiss an employee. She was a sweet woman but had not been an asset to our company. She had dealt with an injury for a few years and was in constant pain. Knowing that she hurt all the time, I overlooked things that should have been addressed during her employment. The time came when our customers began to complain about her, and I knew I had to make a move.

The day I went in to inform her that she no longer had a job, she turned on me like a wild animal. She voiced a lot of things out loud that stung me. But the one thing that shook my whole being was when she told me that I shouldn't call myself a Christian. WHAT? I silently asked God to stabilize me, because I wanted to run, hide, and quit my job. I managed to stay calm only because He was helping me. After several more emotional outbursts, she finally gathered her personal belongings and left. And I fell to pieces.

Her harsh words affected me deeply. I knew that she was hurting and was only reacting to that hurt, but it didn't make her bitter words any easier to take. If I had to sum up in one sentence all that came out of her mouth that day, it would be this: "You have hurt me, and I don't trust you."

My integrity had been questioned, and that's what bothered me the most. I spent many hours going over and over the events of that day with the Lord. I pleaded and begged Him to expose anything in me that was not of Him. I have to say it took me a while to work through it all. Slowly but surely, the faithfulness of God got me through the flashbacks of that day.

Can you recall a time when your integrity was questioned?

_____

_____

How did it make you feel?

_____

_____

> The man of integrity walks securely, but he who takes crooked paths will be found out. (Proverbs 10:9)

The Proverbs 31 woman puts her trust in the Lord and her paths are made straight.

> Trust in the LORD with all your heart and lean not on your own understanding; in all your ways acknowledge him, and he will make your paths straight. (Proverbs 3:5–6)

One thing we can be sure of is that the Lord's integrity is never in question. He is good all the time! So doesn't it make sense that when we follow Him and His teachings, we will also show good to others. In Paul's letter to Titus, he said "In your teaching show integrity, seriousness and soundness of speech that cannot be condemned, so that those who oppose you may be ashamed because they have nothing bad to say about [you ... me]." (Titus 2:7–8). Allow me to paraphrase and speak for the apostle directly to you. "Live your life with such integrity that when people oppose you, they are ashamed because they have nothing bad to say about you." That is exactly what I want my life to look like.

Now, what about the times we mess up? Then we repent and move forward. I have let the past weigh me down way too many times. Satan has attempted to and has been successful in getting a foothold in my thoughts more than I care to admit. God will faithfully convict us when we have wronged another person, and He will reveal to us when we are being deceived by the enemy.

Read Psalm 37:3–6 in your Bible. What does this passage say in your own words?

_____

_____

Our virtuous woman had the full confidence of her husband because he trusted her. Her reliance on the Lord to "**make** [her] righteousness shine like the dawn and the justice of [her] cause like the noonday sun" was evident because she delighted herself in the Lord and was committed to Him. Her husband knew what he had in her was rare; therefore, she was of great value to him.

One last question: Do you think the Lord trusts you? Why or why not?

_____

_____

He trusted a Moabitess named Ruth to the point of including her in the bloodline of Christ, because He knew that she would be faithful to follow Him in obedience. This description from *The Path* blog helps explain just how radical this trust was:

> Most Moabites were polytheist (idolaters) who worshiped many gods and goddesses, but they were widely referred to by the Israelites as "the people of Chemosh" (Numbers 21:29, Judges 11:24).
>
> Chemosh most likely means destroyer, subdue or fish god, and was the Moabites national deity that they honored with horribly cruel rites much like those of Molech, to whom children were sacrificed in fire (2 Kings 3:26-27)....
>
> The Moabites were such devoted followers of Chemosh that they developed a common practice which was to send their daughters out to cultivate friendly relations with the Israelites in order to entice them to join their idolatrous serves (Numbers 25:2).[5]

I hope this helps you better understand the turn Ruth had made when she joined her mother-in-law on the journey to Bethlehem.

Her husband has full confidence in her and lacks nothing of value. (Proverbs 31:11)

Wrap Up: The virtuous woman is trustworthy. Her husband has full confidence in her because she has proved to be a woman of integrity, and she is valuable to him. She commits herself to the ways of the Lord and lives her life in the fullness of His counsel. Because she trusts in Him, others can trust in her.

Spend some time in prayer. Use the space below to make some notes. Whatever He has brought to your mind during this lesson, address it with Him. He is listening.

_____

_____

_____

_____

Endnotes:

[1] Donna, "My Walk with 'Ruth,'" The Path (blog), March 17, 2011, https://dshiflett.wordpress.com/2011/03/17/my-walk-with-ruth/.

[2] Ibid.

[3] The American Heritage Dictionary, Second College Edition, s.v. "trust."

[4] The American Heritage Dictionary, Second College Edition, s.v. "trustworthy."

[5] Donna, "My Walk with 'Ruth.'"

She Is Committed, Loving, and Submissive

PROVERBS 31:12

As I think of our verse for today, I visualize this mighty warrior advancing in battle. The battlefield is tumultuous. The enemy is armed and dangerous! Jesus described him as a murderer from the beginning (John 8:44) and a thief that comes only to steal and kill and destroy (John 10:10).

KJV	NASB	NIV
She will do him good and not evil all the days of her life.	She does him good and not evil all the days of her life.	She brings him good, not harm, all the days of her life.

The virtuous woman (of noble character) consistently wants God's best for her husband. Her desire is to bless him by her deeds and be a blessing to him by her lifestyle.

Why do you think the Holy Spirit has brought this visual of spiritual warfare to my mind?

_____

_____

We are in a spiritual battle. The battle is between good and evil. Satan desires to keep us from what God wants for us. And believe me, he will come after us.

> Be self-controlled and alert. Your enemy the
> devil prowls around like a roaring lion looking
> for someone to devour. (1 Peter 5:8)

Our virtuous woman was committed to showing good to her husband. Oh, my! Can't you just hear the roar of the adversary walking around her, stalking her with lies, deception, oppression, depression? The battle is real. Satan is out to destroy relationships. One way he accomplishes this is by encouraging strife and unforgiveness between husbands and wives.

An article on *Marriage101.org* offers this theory about the cause of America's crumbling marriage landscape:

> The divorce rate in America is more than 50%,
> which means one in two couples will break up.
> Why is it so high? What is the real reason for
> them to divorce? I think we should look for the
> answer from the American belief. Freedom is
> one of the most important beliefs for America
> and nothing can replace it besides love. When [a
> couple marries], they don't run for long love. If
> they think the love and family can't offer them

happiness and safety, they would choose to divorce. They wouldn't think more about the family or the children because they take themselves as the center. That means they love freedom, not stability. Their dreams are running for their own blessedness.[1]

Oatman and I have struggles in our marriage. Marriage is tough. In certain seasons, it would have been easier to walk away. But if there's one thing Oatman and I agree on: We will see this thing through till death do us part. I call that commitment and a whole lot of stubbornness! Divorce is not part of God's plan for us, so it can't be part of ours.

But the battle still rages, doesn't it? Satan continues to attack in order that he might devour us. I have to agree that his tactics are to tempt us to focus on "putting ourselves in the center." Sad to say, but for many, "their dreams are running for their own blessedness."

I know our virtuous woman experienced spiritual warfare because she was **committed** to her God and to her husband. I don't see her in battle unaware of the enemy or even trying to run away. Remember, she was a woman of strength, courage, and fearlessness. She is aware of the spiritual war that physical eyes can't see. This woman who only wants good for her husband is doing battle! As I think of her, I am reminded of a story that Charles Stanley wrote in *When the Enemy Strikes*:

> The story is told of a little boy who came into his mother's kitchen and announced to her, "That was a good fight."

The mother looked at her little boy. His shirt was torn and dirty; his jeans were ripped at the knee; he had a black eye and a big scrape on his elbow. "What was so good about it?" she asked.

He replied, "I won."[2]

Our woman of valor knows about the good fight of faith (1 Timothy 6:12). She presses in and presses on! She can fight with confidence because she knows she's on the winning side.

You and I may feel like we have come through a spiritual fight with torn, dirty clothes, a black eye, and maybe even a big scrape on our elbow, but we will come through on the winning side!

Our Proverbs 31 woman stands firm because she is clothed in the full armor of God.

Write Ephesians 6:11.

_____

_____

Now finish verse 12.
For our struggle is not against flesh and blood, but against

_____

_____

Who are flesh and blood to you? Is there anyone that you are in conflict with right now?

_____

_____

According to Ephesians 6:12, who is the true enemy?

_____

_____

> Therefore put on the full armor of God, so that
> when the day of evil comes, you may be able to
> stand your ground. (Ephesians 6:13)

The armor of God is: (vv.14–17)
Stand firm then, with the belt of _____ buckled around your waist, with the breastplate of _____ in place, and with your feet fitted with the readiness that comes from the gospel of _____. In addition to all this, take up the _____ ____ _____, with which you can extinguish all the flaming arrows of the evil one. Take the _____ of _____ and the _____ of the _____, which is the word of God.

So, God has given us the weapons that it takes to have victory over the enemy. They are truth, righteousness, peace, faith, salvation and the Word of God. Let's suit up girls; the enemy will be on our heels as we commit to show good to others.

The king's mother wanted her beloved son to find a wife that would be committed to him. She also wanted him to find love. The love that says, "I put you ahead of me."

From Romans 12:10–21, make a list of what it means to **love**. Love must be sincere.

_____   _____   _____
_____   _____   _____
_____   _____   _____
_____   _____   _____

Our Proverbs 31 woman was committed, loving, and **submissive**. Doesn't submission show weakness, kinda like being a pushover? NO WAY! It's just the opposite. It takes great strength to submit. Let's explore this. I love how author Kevin Miller explains it:

> The word submit is surely one of the most difficult, disliked, and divisive words in the Bible. But Paul says to these Christians (Ephesians 5), "Submit to one another out of reverence for Christ."
>
> Take, for example, wives and husbands. In Paul's day, a wife had no legal rights. Husbands ... had the financial advantages and virtually all the education. They had the support of pagan philosophy, which taught that women are damaged, inferior forms of males.
>
> Whenever there's this kind of imbalance of power, what's the person holding greater power or authority likely to do? Lord it over the other person, control her, use her to make his life

easier. And what's the person holding less power or authority likely to do? Resist, rebel, make the husband's life miserable in some way.

But Paul offers a better solution, a way to move beyond power struggles. It's called submission. He says, in effect, "In life, when you're in a place of less authority and power" – which in his day included wives, children and slaves – "don't resist and resent and rebel. Out of reverence for Christ, respect and honor and work hard at pleasing the other person. And when you're in a place of more power" – which in Paul's day included husbands, parents, and slave masters – "don't lord it over the other person. Don't use them to make your life easier. Instead, use your power to benefit them."[3]

In the book of Ruth, Orpah turned back to Moab. She went back to her people and gods. Ruth was, on the other hand, determined to remain with Naomi.

Fill in the blanks from Ruth 1:16–17.
But Ruth replied, "Don't urge me to _____ you or to turn back from you. Where you go ____ _____ _____, and where you stay ____ _____ _____. Your people will be my people and your _____ _____ _____. Where you die I will die, and there I will be buried. May the LORD deal with me, be it ever so severely, if anything but death separates you and me."

Scripture tells us that when Naomi realized that Ruth was determined, she stopped urging her to go back, and the two women went on until they came to Bethlehem.

How did Ruth show in Ruth 1:16–17 the attributes of:

Commitment:

_____

_____

Love:

_____

_____

Submission:

_____

_____

King Lemuel's mother desired her son to marry this kind of woman. She would bring him good, not harm, not just one day or a year, but "all the days of her life." There's no doubt that the level of commitment, love, and submission the king's mother described is deep. Ruth shows us what this looks like.

Self-Reflection Time:
What or who have you determined that you are committed to?

_____

_____

Is your level of commitment like Ruth's? Go back and read Ruth 1:16–17 again before explaining your answer.

_____

_____

On the scale below, rate how well you love based on Romans 12:10–21. One represents "I obviously don't get this love thing." Ten represents "I have this love thing mastered."

1 2 3 4 5 6 7 8 9 10

Lastly, submission. How easy is it for you to submit? Be honest.

_____

_____

**She brings him good, not harm all the
days of her life. (Proverbs 31:12)**

Wrap Up: The virtuous woman suits up in the full armor of God and moves forward in the spiritual battle. She triumphs in strength, courage, and fearlessness over the enemy as she is determined to commit, love, and submit to God and others. She brings her husband good, not harm, all the days of her life.

What do you want to say to the Lord today?

_____

_____

Remember, it is the Lord who makes us into the virtuous woman through our dependence on Him. Commit, love, and submit to God!

Endnotes:
[1]Marriage101.org, marriage 101.org/divorce-rates-in-america/.
[2]*When The Enemy Strikes: The Keys to Winning Your Spiritual Battles*, Charles F. Stanley (Nashville: Thomas Nelson, 2004), 21.
[3]Kevin A. Miller, "What's So Scary About Submission?" Today's Christian Woman, September 2008, http://www.todayschristianwoman.com/articles/2008/september/whats-so-scary-about-submission.html.

She Is Hard Working
and Cheerful

PROVERBS 31:13

I believe it is time for us to be reminded of God's watchful care over His children. Sometimes I feel so alone, but a certain verse reminds me that I am absolutely not. It reminds me of God's grip on me, and some days I need that reminder as much as I need the air I breathe. The verse I'm speaking of is:

> "See, I have engraved you on the palms of my hands; your walls are ever before me." (Isaiah 49:16)

Let's do an exercise together. Put an object nearby in your hand. (Nothing sharp please!) Now close your hand and squeeze it as hard as you can and hold. Depending on the object you chose, you may have indentions in your palm as you open your hand. Either way, does it give you a visual of the hold God has on you? You are engraved in the palm of His hands.

> "I give them eternal life, and they shall never perish; no one can snatch them out of my hand." (John 10:28)

Today has been a tough day. My flesh is weak and I feel like God is a thousand miles away. So I have to hold on to what I have been promised. I don't feel Him holding me tightly, and to be honest, I don't feel worthy of His grip on me. But Truth tells me that He is holding onto me whether I feel it or not. Though grateful, I ask why? The answer is His unexplainable love with grace and mercy unimaginable for the worst of sinners—me.

I share this with you because we are studying the Proverbs 31 woman, and I feel so far removed from her. But I am praying that God will change me. How about you? You and I have to remember that we are works in progress. Paul's confession gives me so much encouragement:

> Not that I have already obtained all this, or have already been made perfect, but I press on to take hold of that for which Christ Jesus took hold of me. Brothers [or sisters], I do not consider myself yet to have taken hold of it. But one thing I do: Forgetting what is behind and straining toward what is ahead, I press on toward the goal to win the prize for which God has called me heavenward in Christ Jesus. (Philippians 3:12–14)

KJV	NASB	NIV
She seeketh wool, and flax, and worketh willingly with her hands.	She looks for wool and flax and works with her hands in delight.	She selects wool and flax and works with eager hands.

We left Ruth in the last lesson committing, loving, and submitting to Naomi, but ultimately to God. Whether Ruth professed her faith in Israel's God at that time or whether she was stating what she had already committed to, we don't know. We do know that her actions were only following what her mind and heart had already decided. Ruth saw someone in Naomi that she had to have for herself.

As I previously mentioned, the custom of her country was to worship many gods and goddesses. But seeing the one true and living God in Naomi moved her to repentance and dependence upon Him. Her step of faith, believing Him at His Word, advanced her forward in strength, courage, and fearlessness.

When Naomi and Ruth arrived at Bethlehem, the whole town was stirred because of them. "The women exclaimed, 'Can this be Naomi?'" (Ruth 1:19).

Ten years had passed. The aging process had not been paused just for Naomi. Also, Naomi had experienced great loss; therefore, the sadness in her heart must have shown on her face through lines and expressions. Or just maybe the women were surprised to see her after all those years. One thing we are sure of is that Naomi was a bitter woman. She told the women not to call her "pleasant one" (Naomi) but to call her "bitter" (Mara). I feel so sorry for her as I ponder this section of Scripture. Can you even imagine the pain of losing a husband and two children? It seems more than any woman could bear.

Write Ruth 1:21. I realize our virtuous woman is Ruth, but we have to examine the condition of Naomi to see the character of Ruth.

_____

_____

Who was the Sovereign One in Naomi's eyes?_____

I believe this says so much about Naomi. She appeared to be blaming God for her loss, but she had also heard that God had come to the aid of His people. She certainly knew who was in charge! God understood her broken heart. Though she obviously was not aware of it, He was loving her through Ruth.

Write Ruth 2:2.

_____

_____

Ruth wasted no time in looking for work. She found herself, with Naomi's permission, in the field belonging to Boaz, a relative of Naomi's late husband, Elimelech. Here's our hardworking girl gleaning behind the harvesters in Boaz's field.

Gleaning was the process of gathering grain or other produce left in the fields by reapers. The Old Testament Law required that property owners leave the leftovers (gleanings) of their produce in the fields so they might be gathered by the "poor and the strangers" (Leviticus 19:9-10). Ruth would have fallen into both of these categories. Gleaning was no easy task. It was a backbreaking job. We see from verse 7 that Ruth worked steadily except for a short break. Ruth was not only a hard worker, but she also didn't complain about the work. Ruth said to the foreman, "Please let me glean and gather among the sheaves behind the harvesters." The foreman told Boaz, "She went into the field and has worked steadily from morning till now, except for a short rest in the shelter." (Ruth 2:7)

Based on what we know about Naomi and the state she was in, what does Ruth's godly character convey to us?

_____

_____

As you recall, Ruth had also lost her husband. She, too, was grieving, but she put Naomi ahead of herself. I wonder if her stomach was in knots as she set out to find work soon after arriving in this unfamiliar town and country. I wonder if she prayed, pleading for His favor and protection to be with her as she put one foot in front of another. Remember, she wouldn't have known anybody, plus she was a Moabitess—a Gentile. When she found work in a dirty field, Ruth set to her work steadily without any sign of complaining.

Our Proverbs 31 woman fixed her mind to making selections of wool and flax, then she works with eager hands. According to *The Bible Knowledge Commentary*, "With eager hands is literally 'with the delight of her hands', suggesting that she enjoys her work."[1]

Write Colossians 3:23.

_____

_____

How does our Proverbs 31 woman live out this verse? You can either think of your own Proverbs 31 woman or use Ruth as your example.

_____

_____

Now write Hebrews 6:10.

_____

_____

Who was Ruth helping?_____

Naomi loved her daughter-in-law, and I'm sure she was so grateful for Ruth. But who does not forget your effort as you work hard to help others because of your love for Him? _____

God sees you, dear sibling. We must do the work because we love Him.

**She selects wool and flax and works with
eager hands. (Proverbs 31:13)**

Wrap Up: The virtuous woman works hard and enjoys her work. She is cheerful without any sign of complaining.

What do you need to say to God today?

_____

_____

Endnotes:
[1] *The Bible Knowledge Commentary* (Old Testament), eds. John S. Walvoord and Roy B. Zuck (Colorado Springs: David C. Cook, 1985).

She Knows How to Invest

Before we begin today, allow me the privilege of praying for you.

Dear God, for the one who is reading these words, I ask You to guide and direct her study today. I ask You to speak directly to her in a personal way so that without a doubt, she will know that it is You speaking. Lord, because she has chosen this study, she is open to Your direction for becoming the woman You made her to be, so give her a glimpse of the sanctifying work You are doing in her. Encourage and fill her as she is willing to live a life depending on Your power and recognizing Your grace. In the name that is above all names, Jesus. Amen.

KJV	NASB	NIV
She is like the merchants' ships; she bringeth her food from afar.	She is like merchant ships; she brings her food from afar.	She is like the merchant ships, bringing her food from afar.

Today we will examine how we are investing our time, money, and efforts. The word invest has seven different definitions according to *Webster's New World Dictionary*. Let's look at two of the definitions:

"invest: 5. to put [money] into business, stocks, bonds, etc., for the purpose of obtaining a profit 6. to spend or pay [time, money, etc.] with the expectations of some satisfaction." [1]

Think about these definitions and make a list of how you are currently investing for yourself and/or your family. To help your brain think faster, consider these questions before making your list. How are you spending your time/money or saving your money? In what ways are you finding satisfaction in the care of your home?

_____

_____

_____

_____

You may not think your list quite lives up to "She is like the merchant ships, bringing her food from afar" (Proverbs 31:14). Oh, but it does. Several months ago, my Bible study group studied Proverbs 31. The day we studied verse 14, we went around the room and made our list verbally. One dear sister shared that she had gone the day before to a yard sale and purchased work jeans for her husband for one dollar a pair, and she was able to get several pairs! Another had hit a sale at a local clothing store. Another had made a conscious effort recently to cook more and eat out less. These are all great ways to obtain a profit that will bring satisfaction. I wish I could hear your list or look over your shoulder to see what you have written down. But be assured, I was cheering you on as you were compiling your list.

I am not a coupon clipper or a yard sale shopper, but I do shop for bargains. I love consignment stores, although I don't go very often, which leads me to the number one investment that I make for my husband (since we are empty nesters). I look in my closet and say "enough is enough!" I don't have lots of clothes or shoes, although I love them. I don't have a lot because I don't need a lot. There was a day when shopping was a priority for me. But during those days, I bought mostly on credit and got in over my head in debt. I have sweet freedom by saying "enough is enough." I am totally serious when I say I literally have five pairs of dress pants for work and church, and a couple pair of jeans. Would I like more? Of course, but I don't need them. I have enough.

King Lemuel's mother desired her son to find a coupon clipper, yard sale entrepreneur ... a wise shopper and provider for her husband and children. She wanted him to be blessed by this woman who would prioritize the overall best interest of her family, which would definitely affect him positively.

In what ways would her investments affect her husband positively?

_____

_____

Write Proverbs 21:5.

_____

_____

Now write Proverbs 14:23.

_____

_____

Today, we see from Ruth how hard work brought her profit. Boaz noticed her.

> So Boaz said to Ruth, "My daughter, listen to me.
> Don't go and glean in another field and don't go
> away from here. Stay here with my servant girls.
> Watch the field where the men are harvesting,
> and follow along after the girls. I have told the
> men not to touch you. And whenever you are
> thirsty, go and get a drink from the water jars the
> men have filled." (Ruth 2:8–9)

Not only was Ruth in a strange place, but she was in great danger. It would not have been uncommon for the servant girls to be physically attacked. Also, Boaz told Ruth to drink from the water jars that the men filled. These would have been the household jars, not the ones that the servants would have drunk from. I dearly love how God showed Ruth favor through Boaz. Ruth's hard work was an investment of her time and resources. She was poor and probably felt like she didn't have much to give, but she stepped out and did all she could do and God blessed her. He provided for her and protected her in an unsafe place.

Our world today is in total chaos. Heinous crimes are becoming more and more common. Drug, alcohol, and pornography addictions continue to rise. A woman in our area beat her boyfriend to death with a baseball bat this week. The news anchor said that it was alcohol related. Evil prevails in our communities. But God, just like He did for Ruth, provides and protects us.

How do you feel or not feel provided for right now?

_____

_____

How do you feel or not feel protected right now?

_____

_____

For the remainder of this lesson we will focus on Psalm 91. Turn in your Bibles to this beautiful psalm.

Read verses 3–10 and summarize what God will do for the one who takes refuge in Him.

_____

_____

There is nothing to fear when we take refuge in God. Nothing.

What do you need saving from? _____

Surely he will save me from (fill in the blank)_____

He will save you from even that when you make the Most High your dwelling.

Write Psalm 91:11.

_____

_____

With the Most High as your dwelling, your shelter, your safe place, He will command the angels concerning you. They will lift you up in their hands, and the impossible makes the turn because all things are possible with Him.

The Proverbs 31 woman found her shelter in the Most High. She trusted Him at His Word. She made her investments into His kingdom by caring for those entrusted to her. Sounds like the same advice King Lemuel's mother gave her son, doesn't it?

God promised Israel that when He brought them back from captivity that He would "refresh the weary and satisfy the faint" (Jeremiah 31:25). He will do the same for us dear sister.

Write Psalm 91:14-16.

_____

_____

God says "I will rescue you; I will protect you; I will answer you; I will be with you in trouble; I will deliver you and honor you because you love Me and you find rest in Me."

She is like the merchant ships, bringing her food from afar. (Proverbs 31:14)

Wrap Up: The virtuous woman shows wisdom in how she invests for her family with time, money, and effort. She makes God her Most High, her shelter, as she steps out in faith to provide for her family.

Write out a prayer.

_____

_____

_____

_____

ENDNOTES:

[1] *Webster's New World Dictionary*, Concise Ed., s.v. "invest."

Royal Reflection

It's college basketball tournament time, and that means at our house we are watching lots of basketball. Yesterday Oatman and I watched two teams battle it out to the end. The score stayed close the entire game. There were 3.2 seconds left on the clock and a time-out was called from the team that was two points behind. The cameras moved in on the team huddled up with their coach, getting their last game plan. They could tie it or win the game, but they only had 3.2 seconds in which to pull it off.

Oatman and I were on the edge of our seats as we waited for their time-out to end. Obviously we couldn't hear what was being said, but my imagination took over. I said to my basketball partner, my husband, "The coach is telling the young man he has chosen to take the last shot. That's so much pressure, but what an honor!"

Immediately the Holy Spirit gave me a visual. Stay with me here. Picture a group of followers huddled up with Jesus, getting the "game plan." Just like the coach, Jesus is looking into individual faces as He speaks and instructs. Just like the coach did in yesterday's game, Jesus looks at the chosen shooter and says, "You are the one to take the shot. Now, let's do this thing!" Then all the tight fists of the followers come up as they vow to stand and work together.

Imagine you are one of the huddle participants. Jesus is looking directly at you and telling you to "take the shot" because He trusts in you to do this certain thing at this certain time. Maybe He has picked you to teach a class at church, volunteer at a local charity, leave your current job to go to another, or maybe you are called to stay home full-time to raise your child in the ways of the Lord. Whatever it is that Jesus has called you to, do you consider it an honor or are you discouraged by it? He has chosen you! You are the one He has picked to "take this shot" in the last seconds before His return. What will be your response?

She Is a Leader

PROVERBS 31:15

I know this sounds very elementary, but all it takes to be a leader is to have a follower. We have all led someone some time or another; therefore, we are all leaders. You may consider yourself a bad, good, or maybe even a great leader. I am blessed to have known great leaders in my lifetime.

Whether or not you consider yourself a leader, believe me when I say, you are leading someone. The question is, how are you leading?

I'm sure, like me, you have been blessed to know some great leaders. My mother, for one, taught our family about integrity in many areas of life. Mother has always been an energetic hard worker on the job as well as at home.

Last week we had a winter storm with freezing rain, sleet, and snow that paralyzed our town for a couple of days. Only a few businesses were open. My sister Robin and I were discussing how hard it was for so many people to get to their jobs. She remembered and shared with me how our mother would walk a few miles to work when the roads were too bad to drive on. We both agreed how thankful we are to have a mother that led us with such an example as that.

I am not a workaholic by any stretch of the imagination, but I go to work to work. I hope that I have set an example for my kids to mimic like my mother, who showed our family how to lead with integrity. Our Proverbs 31 woman did the same!

KJV	NASB	NIV
She riseth also while it is yet night, and giveth meat to her household, and a portion to her maidens.	She rises also while it is still night and gives food to her household and portions to her maidens.	She gets up while it is still dark; she provides food for her family and portions for her servant girls.

Name a few great leaders that you have known.

_____

In your opinion, what traits does a great leader have?

_____

Three things stand out to me in Proverbs 31:15.
- She prepares herself.
- She plans ahead.
- She delegates.

How do you think she prepares herself?

_____

_____

Write Mark 1:35.

_____

_____

I realize Scripture does not say that she gets up while it is still dark to pray. But let's not forget that she is a woman who fears the Lord! And another thing to consider is what it takes to be this woman ... power, the kind of power that resurrected our Savior.

> ... His incomparably great power for us who
> believe. That power is like the working of his
> mighty strength, which he exerted in Christ
> when he raised him from the dead and seated
> him at his right hand in the heavenly realms.
> (Ephesians 1:19-20)

I believe she sought the Lord early in her day so that His power was like the working of his mighty strength within her.

Write Deuteronomy 34:12.

_____

_____

This was the last verse contributed to Moses, who was a great leader of Israel. The same power with Moses is in all of us who believe.

The Proverbs 31 woman prepared herself to face her day by seeking God and His leadership over her because He was the Lord of her life.

> Prepare your minds for action; be self-controlled
> ... As obedient children, do not conform to the
> evil desires you had when you lived in ignorance.
> But just as he who called you is holy, so be holy
> in all you do; for it is written: "Be holy, because I
> am holy." (1 Peter 1:13–16)

She also planned ahead.

How do you think she planned ahead?

_____

_____

I have learned that if I do not plan supper before I leave for work in the morning, I will be throwing hot dogs in the microwave or a frozen pizza in the oven when I get home. Providing for a family takes planning ahead. How does the old saying go? "Plan your work and work your plan!" So true.

Besides her family, who else does Proverbs 31:15 say were entrusted to her? _____

God says, "For I know the plans I have for you ... plans to prosper you and not to harm you, plans to give you hope and a future" (Jeremiah 29:11). Before you arrived here on planet Earth, He had planned for you. He not only planned for your arrival, but also for your life!

Our virtuous woman prepared herself early in her day; she was a planner and she also delegated the responsibilities.

Who did she delegate work to?_____

Of course, she delegated work to her servants which would take planning.

Do you delegate well? Why or why not.

_____

_____

Let's look in on Scripture to see how to delegate. We will actually be learning from Jethro, Moses' father-in-law. Read Exodus 18.

Jethro said what Moses was doing was not good. Write Exodus 18:18.

_____

_____

What steps did he give Moses in order to delegate? (vv. 19–22)

_____

_____

_____

Is God bringing something to your mind that you can delegate to make your work lighter?

If so, what are the steps you will take?

Sometimes we try to be superwomen and take on all the work ourselves. You and I can't do all the work! It's okay to delegate. It's actually what great leaders do! Years ago I had a boss who told me once, "Kathy, you are working very hard, but are you working smart?" He was referring to a project that I was working on that wasn't getting done because I was not delegating some of the work to talented team members. A light bulb went off in my head, and I immediately enlisted their help, and we completed the work together.

King Lemuel's mother led her son in the fear of the Lord. As king, he had followers, which made him an important leader. Her desire for her son in his helpmate was someone who would lead well, which included preparing herself, planning ahead, and delegating work. With each verse we study, I feel like we are still getting to know our king's mother better, don't you?

She gets up while it is still dark; she provides food for her family and portions for her servant girls. (Proverbs 31:15)

Wrap Up: Our virtuous woman is a great leader. She prepares herself as she gives her day to the Lord each morning, asking for His guidance and instruction. She has much responsibility that requires preplanning; therefore, she thinks ahead to plan her work then she works her plan. She knows that she can't do all the work alone, so she delegates what she can to make her load lighter.

Think about how you are preparing, planning, and delegating in this present season. Talk to God about the thing He has given you to do. Remember, out of all the women that He could have picked, He picked you!

She Perseveres

PROVERBS 31:16

You may be thinking that we have left our Ruth behind. Not a chance! Let's catch up with her in the fields belonging to Boaz. As you recall, Ruth found favor through Boaz. He told Ruth to stay in his fields to glean. He protected her from the men who could have harmed her. And he showed her kindness by offering her water from the household jars. Ruth is taken aback by the favor Boaz has shown her. She bows down before him and exclaims, "Why have I found such favor in your eyes that you notice me—a foreigner?" (Ruth 2:10).

Write Ruth 2:11.

_____

_____

How did Ruth show perseverance?

_____

_____

There are several verses in the book of James where we see this word perseverance in the NIV. It's patience in the King James translation. The Greek word for patience means "endurance." To endure means "to stand firm," "to stay behind."[1]

KJV	NASB	NIV
She considereth a field, and buyeth it; with the fruit of her hands she planteth a vineyard.	She considers a field and buys it; from her earnings she plants a vineyard.	She considers a field and buys it; out of her earnings she plants a vineyard.

Our Proverbs 31 woman considered a field, bought it, and out of her earnings planted a vineyard. Sounds neat and clean, doesn't it? NOT! Life happened between the three things she did. It could have been years between the steps that she took.

Answer the following questions based on your own life experiences or someone else's:

What goes into considering a major purchase like buying a house or a business? Don't forget the emotional and mental aspect of making the decision.

_____

_____

After the decision is made to buy it, what's the process?

_____

_____

Her investment paid off. Maybe this happened quickly or maybe not. If you have experienced the ups and downs of being a business owner, you know exactly where I'm going with this. Oatman and I owned a business for five years, and there were days when I didn't know if I was going to make it or not. In our virtuous woman's case, it paid off eventually, but what are some things she might have had to endure?

_____

_____

She took her earnings and planted a vineyard. Again we see our virtuous woman taking another step in providing for her family.

Do you think the process was an easy one? Explain your answer.

_____

_____

Boaz told Ruth, "I've been told **all** about what you have done for your mother-in-law since the death of your husband" (Ruth 2:11, emphasis added). Sounds like Ruth kept going day in and day out, doesn't it? Today the words "your husband" stuck out to me. I believe God wants us to realize Ruth pressed on and persevered to care for her mother-in-law even at a grievous time for her.

Think about Naomi and her losses, a husband and two children.

What are some ways that Ruth might have helped Naomi before arriving in Bethlehem?

_____

_____

Ruth obviously knew what it meant to persevere. You understand perseverance when you get up every morning, putting one foot in front of another, and you keep going in spite of everything life throws your way.

> We can rejoice too, when we run into problems
> and trials for we know that they are good for us
> — they help us learn to be patient. And patience
> develops strength of character in us and helps us
> trust God more each time we use it until finally
> our hope and faith are strong and steady. Then,
> when that happens, we are able to hold our heads
> high no matter what happens and know that all
> is well, for we know how dearly God loves us,
> and we feel this warm love everywhere within us
> because God has given us the Holy Spirit to fill
> our hearts with his love. (Romans 5:3-5 TLB)

Consider Ruth. Personalize the passage above to what we know about her thus far.

_____

_____

Now, personalize the passage to your life. What is God trying to tell you?

_____

_____

Perseverance [patience] must finish its work so that we may be mature and complete, not lacking anything. (James 1:4)

How long does it take? A lifetime. In patience we endure and we see it through. It takes standing firm, and it feels so often we are staying behind. However, if we stay the course, living in obedience to God, we become mature and complete.

> Blessed is the man who perseveres under trial, because when he has stood the test, he will receive the crown of life that God has promised to those who love him. (James 1:12)

> **She considers a field and buys it; out of her earnings she plants a vineyard. (Proverbs 31:16)**

Wrap Up: Our virtuous woman stands firm in her reliance on God, and she perseveres through the ups and downs of life. She knows that patience will develop strength of character in her, and it will help her trust God more each time she uses it until finally her hope and faith will be strong and steady.

What are you currently enduring with patience?

_____

_____

Allow God to help you. Talk to Him about your situation. Be encouraged that God is doing a sanctifying work in you!

Endnotes:
[1]James Strong, *The Strongest Strong's Exhaustive Concordance of the Bible*, eds. John R. Kohlenberger and James A. Swanson (Grand Rapids, MI: Zondervan, 2001).

She Takes Care of Herself

PROVERBS 31:17

This may be the hardest lesson to write thus far. Why, you ask? Because the conviction from my lack of concern for my own health is already setting in. I allow the busyness of life to drive me most days. I get exhausted and then fail to let my health be a priority, and it suffers. I tell myself that starting tomorrow, I will eat more nutritional foods, exercise, and not let stress get the best of me. This becomes a focus until life happens and other things replace it. It's overwhelming most days to pull it all together. But we have a responsibility to care for our bodies because our bodies house the Spirit of the living God.

> Don't you know that you yourselves are God's temple and that God's Spirit lives in you? If anyone destroys God's temple, God will destroy him; for God's temple is sacred, and you are that temple. (1 Corinthians 3:16-17)

Our Proverbs 31 woman, using Ruth as our example, had energy and strength to aid her in completing her work. I'm sure there were days that she failed to balance life like she should, but her body was strong and healthy. We can know this because of all she accomplished.

KJV	NASB	NIV
She girdeth her loins with strength, and strengtheneth her arms.	She girds herself with strength and makes her arms strong.	She sets about her work vigorously; her arms are strong for her tasks.

I have been on staff at my church for two years. Prior to that, I was an area supervisor of women's fitness centers in Kentucky, Missouri, and Illinois. During those ten years in the fitness industry, I was very conscious of my health. Working out and eating healthy was a lifestyle for me. In contrast, my day as a church secretary is mostly sedentary. I also get to enjoy potlucks and gifts of cookies, pies, and other sweet treats. Just this week, our luncheon after Bible study included fried chicken, mashed potatoes and cake. Believe me, it was delicious, and I delighted in every bite. Taking care of Kathy is not always a priority, but my body is a temple of God, and that will never change.

Write 1 Corinthians 6:19–20.

_____

_____

What does it mean to you to be the temple in which the Holy Spirit of God resides?

_____

_____

What does this stir in you?
- Believing but not understanding
- Never thought about it until now
- Heart filled with thankfulness
- Other_____

How are you honoring God with your body?

_____

_____

After the Israelites left their captivity in Egypt, God took care of them in the wilderness. He fed them, protected them, and told them how they were to live by the laws He established. Then He called on His people to build the tabernacle. There was great care given to its design. Let's look at why.

Write Exodus 25:1–2, 8–9.

_____

_____

_____

_____

What was Moses to have the Israelites do?

_____

_____

They were to make a structure and all its furnishings exactly like the pattern that God would show them.

The two names used for the structure were sanctuary and tabernacle.

The Hebrew word *miqdas* for sanctuary means "holy place."[1] Tabernacle, *miskan*, means "a dwelling place."[1] The tabernacle was the holy place in which God chose to dwell with His people. When the tabernacle was readied for service, God's presence filled it.

> Then the cloud covered the Tent of Meeting, and the glory of the LORD filled the tabernacle. Moses could not enter the Tent of Meeting because the cloud had settled upon it, and the glory of the LORD filled the tabernacle. In all the travels of the Israelites, whenever the cloud lifted from above the tabernacle, they would set out; but if the cloud did not lift, they did not set out—until the day it lifted. So the cloud of the LORD was over the tabernacle by day, and fire was in the cloud by night, in the sight of all the house of Israel during all their travels. (Exodus 40:34-38)

Take a few minutes and glance at Exodus 25 through Exodus 30:21. Notice the headings and instruction to "make," all very specific according to God's design. God also gave King David a pattern for the temple. Although David was not to build it, because he was a man of war, he gathered the needed supplies so that Solomon, his son, God's chosen, could build the temple.

Read 1 Chronicles 29:1–5.

The temple was furnished with such greatness because it was to be the house of God. When it was completed, the Ark of the Covenant was moved in, and God's presence filled the temple.

> When the priests withdrew from the Holy Place, the cloud filled the temple of the LORD. And the priests could not perform their service because of the cloud, for the glory of the LORD filled his temple. (1 Kings 8:10–11)

God in all his wisdom designed the tabernacle, temple, and our bodies. All when given to Him would be filled with His presence.

Meditate on these facts about your body:

- "In the average adult, the skin covers about 20 square feet and weighs about 10 pounds."[2]
- "There are more than 600 individual skeletal muscles in the human body."[3]
- "An adult skeleton has 206 bones."[4]
- "There are about 9,000 taste buds on the surface of the tongue, in the throat, and on the roof of the mouth. Taste buds contain chemoreceptors that respond to chemicals from food and other substances that are dissolved by the saliva in the mouth."[5]
- "The body carries about 25 trillion red blood cells, the most abundant cells in the body. Red blood cells make up about 45% of blood's volume."[6]
- "Every hour, about 180 million newly formed red blood cells enter the bloodstream."[7]
- "The circulatory system of arteries, veins, and capillaries is about 60,000 miles long."[8]
- "The heart beats more than 2.5 billion times in an average lifetime."[9]

- "In a healthy adult, the small intestine can range between 18 and 23 feet long, about four times longer than the person is tall. About 90% of the body's nutrients are absorbed into the bloodstream in the small intestine."[10]
- "Hundreds of billions of neurons carry electrical signals that control the body from the brain and the spinal cord."[11]
- "Recent estimates suggest that the average adult brain contains approximately 86 billion neurons."[12]

Write Psalm 139:13.

> You are God's design. He chose it, and He Him-
> self did the knitting together of your body. You
> are fearfully and wonderfully made. His works
> are wonderful (Psalm 139:14).

What changes in your lifestyle are you willing to make to take better care for your body, the temple of God?

**She sets about her work vigorously; Her arms
are strong for her tasks. (Proverbs 31:17)**

Wrap Up: Our virtuous woman is mindful that her body is the temple of the living God. She is deliberate in caring for this temple the best she can physically, mentally, emotionally, and spiritually so that she will be strong for the work God has laid out for her.

Tell God what this lesson has stirred up in you. Ask for His help in taking better care of your body!

Endnotes:

[1]James Strong, *The Strongest Strong's Exhaustive Concordance of the Bible*, eds. John R. Kohlenberger and James A. Swanson (Grand Rapids, MI: Zondervan, 2001).

[2]"Integumentary System (Skin)" Innerbody, http://www.innerbody.com/anatomy/integumentary.

[3]Beverly McMillan, *Human Body: A Visual Guide*. (Buffalo: Firefly Books Inc., 2006).

[4]Alexander, R. McNeill, *Human Bones* (New York: Nevraumont Publishing Company, 2005).

[5]National Geographic Society, *The Incredible Machine* (Washington, D.C.: The National Geographic Society, 1986).

[6]Ibid.

[7]Ibid.

[8]Ibid.

[9]"Amazing Heart Facts," NOVA Online, http://www.pbs.org/wgbh/nova/heart/heartfacts.html.

[10]McMillan, *Human Body: A Visual Guide*.

[11]Ibid.

[12]Kendra Cherry, "10 Quick Facts About the Brain," VeryWell, psychology.about.com/od/biopsychology/fl/10-Quick-Facts-About-the-Brain.htm.

She Has Spiritual Eyes

PROVERBS 31:18

Every once in a while in the church office, our pastor will respond to a comment by saying, "That's having eyes to see." We certainly have eyes to see our present circumstances from our point of view, but what my pastor is referring to is seeing from God's perspective.

KJV	NASB	NIV
She perceiveth that her merchandise is good; her candle goeth not out by night.	She senses her gain is good; her lamp does not go out at night.	She sees that her trading is profitable and her lamp does not go out at night.

How might your perspective change if you looked beyond your present circumstances (a job loss, a sick loved one, or maybe a season of expected good things happening) to see from a heavenly perspective?

I took one such opportunity this morning to see a situation through God's eyes. The situation from a human perspective would seem a bit hopeless. But seeing it from God's ... well, I'll just tell you my response: "Oh Lord, You are good!" (And by the way, I couldn't help myself; I made my proclamation out loud!)

I believe Lemuel's mother had eyes to see beyond the present circumstances. Because of the love she had for her son, she desired her son to find a helpmate who would do the same. I think of it this way: I have to wear glasses to help me see. Honestly, my eyes are so bad without my glasses I would not be able to see you even if you walked right up to me. My eyesight is horrible! This can also be the case for our spiritual eyesight. Without the Word of God, just like my sight without my glasses, life would seem hopeless. Our physical eyes see what's in front of us, but spiritual eyes see circumstances through the Word of God. It brings things into focus and helps us distinguish between what is right and wrong and what is good and evil. The Word of God is His voice sharing what He needs for us to know.

Let's face it: We all complain because we choose to see from an earthly perspective, and life here is far from perfect. But we have a perfect God who has the perfect plan for each of us. That alone is cause for a praise shout!

The king's mother told her son to look for a woman who would see her life as profitable.

Do you see your life as profitable?

In what areas?

_____

_____

Have you wondered from God's viewpoint if the areas in your life that you think are profitable truly are? The areas that you feel are your weakest and that you're maybe even unsuccessful in may be the very things that God is about to use to reveal His glory in ways that just might blow your mind.

I want us to practice getting out of our worldly bubble and see from God's vantage point.

Let's pray before we start. _Dear God, I want eyes to see what You see. Help me see the following passages in Your Holy Scripture through Your eyes only. Because I live in this world, I too often see from a worldly perspective. I want that to change in me. But it will only come about as You open my spiritual eyes to see past what my physical eyes detect. Lord, shut out all distractions and remove anything that is obstructing my view of You. Amen._

Read Matthew 8:23–27.

From the disciples' perspective, what did they see and feel?

_____

_____

What did Jesus do?

_____

_____

What was His perspective?

_____

_____

Read Matthew 14:22–33.

What did Peter see from his perspective?

_____

_____

What did Jesus do?

_____

_____

I don't believe Peter doubted Jesus or he wouldn't have ever gotten out of the boat. I believe Peter doubted himself. What did Jesus say to Peter?

_____

_____

Keeping that in mind, what was Jesus' perspective of the situation?

_____

_____

Read Mark 6:30–44.

What was the disciples' perspective of feeding five thousand men, plus women and children?

_____

_____

What happened?

_____

_____

With your worldly perspective removed, what do you see?

_____

_____

In all three of these passages, faith was tested.

What is faith according to Hebrews 11:1?

_____

_____

What does Hebrews 11:6 say about pleasing God?

_____

_____

Faith in our living God and belief in His living Word becomes our spiritual eyes. Because "we live by faith, not by sight" (2 Corinthians 5:7).

Ruth left everything and everyone behind to follow Naomi, entering into the unknown because she knew the God she trusted would protect her and provide for her. Her faith had already been tested and would be tested so much more. But God was more than enough for her to cling to. Nothing or no one she left behind compared to the One she was surrendered to.

I applaud you, dear sister! Great job today! Keep looking to your Lord each day as you do this work and rest assured He is doing what He promised you:

> Being confident of this, that he who began a good
> work in you will carry it on to completion until
> the day of Christ Jesus. (Philippians 1:6)

> **She sees that her trading is profitable, and her
> lamp does not go out at night. (Proverbs 31:18)**

Wrap Up: Our virtuous woman sees beyond her present circumstances of the things life can throw at us because she has a heavenly perspective. Her faith helps her see life through spiritual eyes. God's plan and purpose for her becomes clearer as she trusts her life to Him, applying His Word to her life.

God desires for you to see what He sees. Ask Him to help you. He's waiting!

She Uses Her Skills

PROVERBS 31:19

Our Proverbs 31 woman knew how to use her hands with skill in providing clothing for her family and perhaps others. According to a Bible study reflection from the Middletown Bible Church, "this verse describes a very ancient method of spinning used in the days before the spinning wheel even existed. The distaff was a staff used for holding the flax, tow or wool that would be spun into thread by means of the spindle. The spindle would turn and twist the fibers into threads."[1]

KJV	NASB	NIV
She layeth her hands to the spindle, and her hands hold the distaff.	She stretches out her hands to the distaff, and her hands grab the spindle.	In her hand she holds the distaff and grasps the spindle with her fingers.

This determined, hardworking woman applied herself to the work of spinning and performed it with skill.

A couple of lessons ago I had you glance through Exodus 25–30:21. As you recall, through Moses, the Lord instructed the Israelites to make a tabernacle in the wilderness where His presence would always be with them.

Read Exodus 31:1–11.

This is another example of how God "makes" us, or equips us, for the work He has for us to do.

Fill in the blanks from Exodus 31:2–3. This is God talking, Sister! "See I have _____ Bezalel son of Uri, the son of Hur, of the tribe of Judah, and I have _____ him with the Spirit of God, with _____, _____ and _____ in all kinds of crafts."

I just had a visual. I can see Bezalel surprised by his skill, taking a break every once in a while just to be amazed by the work of his hands. I hope he realized fully that it was the Spirit of God who was blessing him by helping him from start to finish.

I get amazed at how God helps me. I'm serious when I say that some days I look back and am blown away at God because of what I have been able to accomplish.

My friend Lori tells me that He makes her much smarter than she is. She is a professional with a very important job. She works long tiring days. She remembers always to praise God for what is accomplished through her because she says, "Really, I'm not that smart!"

I can certainly relate. I grew up very shy and fearful about everything. I felt insecure, unattractive, and not very smart. God began putting me in leadership roles. Slowly, I began stepping out and stepping into some very uncomfortable places. God helped me in more ways than I can even communicate. He gave me jobs that I wasn't educated for. His favor fell on me and, though uncomfortable, I stepped into the unknown, and He blessed me.

I took risks. Some seemed to prove unsuccessful, but through them, God taught me perseverance and dependence on Him and so much more! So ... even though I considered those unsuccessful times from the perspective of time, money, and effort, I have to ask myself were they truly unsuccessful from God's point of view? It certainly helps me better understand Romans 8:28:

> And we know that in all things God works for
> the good of those who love him, who have been
> called according to his purpose.

All of us have been gifted by God on purpose for a purpose. I have seen for myself that as the seasons of life change, some of my abilities have also changed. For me, one example would be writing this study. I believe with all my heart that this is an assignment by God, so God is filling me with skill, ability, and knowledge to complete it. I have another writing assignment in the future. I know this because he has given me a few details. After that, I don't know. What I am confident in is that He will equip me for whatever He has for me to do.

From the passage in Exodus 31:1–11, God skilled craftsmen for the work He had for them. The same is true for you.

How have you been gifted with specific abilities by God?

_____

_____

Let's explore one more thing today about applying our abilities as God commands.

Read the verses below from Exodus:

> And everyone who was willing and whose heart
> moved him came and brought an offering to the
> LORD for the work on the Tent of Meeting, for all
> its service, and for the sacred garments. All who
> were willing, men and women alike. (Exodus
> 35:21–22)

> And all the women who were willing and had the
> skill spun the goat hair. (Exodus 35:26)

> All the Israelite men and women who were will-
> ing brought to the LORD freewill offerings for
> all the work the LORD through Moses had com-
> manded them to do. (Exodus 35:29)

> Then Moses summoned Bezalel and Oholiab
> and every skilled person to whom the LORD had
> given ability and who was willing to come and do
> the work. (Exodus 36:2)

Do you see a common phrase in these passages? God gave the gifts of skill, ability, and knowledge, but He left it up to the craftsmen to give an offering to the tabernacle and to do the work. "Those who were willing." Allow that to soak in. God called the people and equipped them, but not all were willing to bring an offering and/or to use the abilities God empowered them with.

My mind is trying desperately to move past any examples from my own life, because I feel at this moment my heart would not be able to stand it. I want always to be willing to do whatever the Lord asks of me, but I know I so often fall short of obedience.

If you did not identify your areas where God has gifted you with skill, ability, and knowledge, ask God to reveal that to you. My last question is: Are you willing to give the offering by doing the work assigned to you?

In her hand she holds the distaff and grasps the spindle with her fingers. (Proverbs 31:19)

Wrap Up: Our virtuous woman has identified the areas of her gifts of skill, ability, and knowledge. She is aware that these things in her are supernatural. She is willing to use what God has given her to accomplish what He has commanded.

Spend time in prayer to the One who equips you for all good works. We will spend time with Ruth in our next lesson.

Endnotes:
[1]Middletown Bible Church, "Christian Home and Family: The Virtuous Woman of Proverbs 31," http://www.middletownbiblechurch.org/homefam/pr31text.pdf

Royal Reflection

In 2010, I went to Poland with a team to help with English Day Camps. Thankfully, our schedules permitted a couple of days of sightseeing. One excursion took us to the Wawel Castle, the residence of several Polish princes, in Krakow, Poland.

I was especially starstruck by the massive rooms with exquisite furnishings and extravagant tapestries and artwork. I noticed right away that there were sections of each room that were roped off. I wanted to touch the articles, but my access to them was denied.

As I walked around, I often blocked out the voice of our guide because of the beauty my eyes were trying to take in. The Lord and I began a silent dialog about the privileges of palace living, as well as the responsibilities. He reminded me that the status of my royal lineage of being His daughter granted me full access to Him.

> Let us then approach the throne of grace with
> confidence, so that we may receive mercy and
> find grace to help us in our time of need. (Hebrews 4:16)

I wondered what it would feel like to live in such a place. It may sound silly, but I could almost imagine myself as a resident of the Wawel Castle that day—with no ropes of course! The freedom of feeling at home there in my imagination reminded me that in Christ, I am free to live and serve without any ropes holding me back.

Don't you see, Princess? Your Father, the King, has crowned you for the journey ahead. If you feel roped in or tied down in bondage, it is the enemy tying the knots and pulling on the slack. Move forward in freedom—the freedom that Jesus died to give you.

> It is for freedom that Christ has set us free. Stand firm, then, and do not let yourselves be burdened again by a yoke of slavery. (Galatians 5:1)

She Is Compassionate, Kind, and Generous

PROVERBS 31:20

In our last lesson we saw our priceless woman willingly doing what she was called and equipped to do. Today we will see the attributes of what girded her as she stepped out.

KJV	NASB	NIV
She stretcheth out her hand to the poor; yea, she reacheth forth her hands to the needy.	She extends her hand to the poor, and she stretches out her hands to the needy.	She opens her arms to the poor and extends her hands to the needy.

King Lemuel's mother was a woman of compassion, kindheartedness, and generosity. Look at the instruction she first gave her son on how he should reign as king:

> Speak up for those who cannot speak for themselves, for the rights of all who are destitute.
> Speak up and judge fairly; defend the rights of the poor and needy. (Proverbs 31:8–9)

She told her son to pay attention to those who needed help, then speak up to judge them fairly and defend their rights. I feel her saying, "Oh, my son, you have to choose a bride that is willing to do the same!"

It's time for a quick review of the advice queen mother gave Lemuel in verses 1-9.

- Lemuel's mother spoke words of instruction to her son from a burdened heart because of the vows she had made to the Lord.
- She warned him against women and alcohol which could ruin him and directed him toward doing the will of God.
- From a compassionate heart, Lemuel's mother reminded her son that through obedience to the law of God, people would be taken care of.
- In boldness and confidence, she told her son to be brave and speak up for those who couldn't speak for themselves.

I don't think for a minute that she was the kind of woman that would say, "Don't do as I do, just do as I say." She herself lived out her deep commitment to God with a steadfastness that drew her closer to the One who was faithful in changing her day after day into the perfected woman she was striving to be.

Now, we will look a little closer at three attributes every Proverbs 31 woman possesses, and then we will check in on Ruth. Last time we saw her, she was bowed down with her face to the ground in front of Boaz. Her body only followed what her grateful heart was already doing!

Every Proverbs 31 woman is compassionate, kind and generous. She has sorrow for the sufferings or trouble of others and an urge to help. Her kindness leads her to sympathy, gentleness and unselfish generosity.

As you recall, Elimelech, Naomi, and her two sons, Mahlon and Kilion, moved to Moab to escape a famine in Bethlehem. While in Moab, Mahlon and Kilion married Moabite women, Ruth and Orpah. These women were pagans. In their country of Moab, the custom was to worship false gods.

When the time came that God began to urge Naomi to return to her homeland, she pleaded with her two widowed daughters-in-law to remain with their families in their familiar country. Orpah, with great emotion, agreed to stay with her family and her gods, but Ruth was determined to go to Bethlehem with Naomi.

Write Ruth 1:16–17.

_____

_____

Who was Ruth's God?_____

Naomi's God was the one true living God of Israel, the God who created the universe. The God who created Ruth, created you and me. Yes, that God—our God! Ruth followed her mother-in-law back to Naomi's homeland, but ultimately she was following the God she had surrendered to.

We know from Scripture, Naomi was in a devastating season of her life.

How do we know this? (Ruth 1:20–21)

_____

Ruth set out right away, perhaps the very next day after their arrival, to provide for them.

What did Ruth ask Naomi to let her do? (Ruth 2:2)

_____

_____

> She found herself working in a field belonging to Boaz, who was from the clan of Elimelech. (Ruth 2:3)

Hardworking Ruth only took time from her work for a short rest midday. Boaz noticed Ruth and showed her favor. He told her to stay in his fields to glean and that she would be protected and provided for.

> At this, she bowed down with her face to the ground. She exclaimed, "Why have I found such favor in your eyes that you notice me—a foreigner?" (Ruth 2:10)

Write Ruth 2:11.

_____

_____

In what ways was Ruth compassionate?

_____

_____

In what ways was she kindhearted?

_____

_____

**She opens her arms to the poor and extends
her hands to the needy. (Proverbs 31:20)**

The Proverbs 31 woman not only looked out for her own family, but she kept her eyes and heart open to see the needs of those around her. The Hebrew meaning of extends means "to let go."

We see this woman, who fears the Lord, with her arms open because she feels sorrow for the sufferings or trouble of another and has the urge to help. We see compassion and kindheartedness in Ruth in how she cared for her mother-in-law.

Let's look ahead just briefly to Ruth 2:17–18. Read those verses in your Bible.

How was she a generous person?

_____

_____

Ruth brought back the barley and also part of her lunch to Naomi. Here we see the generosity of Ruth. She extended her hands by "letting go" of what she had to meet a need of another, which just happened to be her mother-in-law.

Wrap Up: Our virtuous woman is compassionate, kind, and generous. She is available and ready to meet the needs of the less fortunate.

Write out a prayer. But before you do, meditate on these words.

> Dear children, let us not love with words or
> tongue but with actions and in truth.
> (1 John 3:18)
>
> Faith by itself, if it is not accompanied by action,
> is dead. (James 2:17)

She Does Not Worry Excessively

PROVERBS 31:21

Our Proverbs 31 woman saw the approaching cold season coming, but had no fear for her household. She was the woman who would read these headlines without fear or excessive worry: "Worst Storm in Decades Batters Jerusalem"[1]

KJV	NASB	NIV
She is not afraid of the snow for her household: for all her household are clothed with scarlet.	She is not afraid of the snow for her household, for all her household are clothed with scarlet.	When it snows, she has no fear for her household; for all of them are clothed in scarlet.

She is not afraid for her family; therefore, those feelings that lead many to excessive worry don't affect her.

According to *Web MD.com*, "Worrying is feeling uneasy or being overly concerned about a situation or problem. With excessive worrying, your mind and body go into overdrive as you constantly focus on "what might happen."[2]

I come from a long line of chronic excessive worriers. The Lord is constantly helping me in this area by reminding me what He says about worry.

This passage is part of the Sermon of the Mount.

"Therefore I tell you, do not worry about your life, what you will eat or drink; or about your body, what you will wear. Is not life more important than food, and the body more important than clothes? Look at the birds of the air; they do not sow or reap or store away in barns, and yet your heavenly Father feeds them. Are you not much more valuable than they? Who of you by worrying can add a single hour to his life?

And why do you worry about clothes? See how the lilies of the field grow. They do not labor or spin. Yet I tell you that not even Solomon in all his splendor was dressed like one of these. If that is how God clothes the grass of the field, which is here today and tomorrow is thrown into the fire, will he not much more clothe you, O you of little faith? So do not worry, saying, 'What shall we eat?' or 'What shall we drink?' or 'What shall we wear?' For the pagans run after all these things, and your heavenly Father knows that you need them. But seek first his kingdom and his righteousness, and all these things will be given to you as well. Therefore do not worry about tomorrow, for tomorrow will worry about itself. Each day has enough trouble of its own."(Matthew 6:25–34)

Fill in the blank: Jesus says:
"Do not _____." Again: "Do not _____." Once more:
"Do not _____."

Jesus told us not to worry. Why?

_____

_____

If your answer included it shows a lack of trust in God, I agree.
Jesus says, "Your heavenly Father will take care of you."

Another reason we shouldn't worry is that it affects our body
in negative ways.

Look at the following list according to *WebMD.com*.[3]

Difficulty swallowing	Muscle tension	Dizziness
Nausea	Dry mouth	Nervous
Rapid breathing	Fast heartbeat	Shortness of breath
Fatigue	Headaches	Sweating
Trembling and twitching		

Or even:

Suppression of the immune system
Digestive disorders
Short-term memory loss
Premature coronary artery disease
Heart attack

The pagans worry and fret and destroy their bodies because they have no hope. But we, children of God, have hope because we know the Savior of the World! He saved us from such things as worry. He says to us, "Do not worry about your life."

I believe it's safe to say that we all worry about something. We all have "worry triggers." When I was a young girl, I worried excessively that something would happen to my mother. I would lie in bed and pray to God to keep my mother alive. This went on for years. It makes me sad as I think about it now. My mother was and still is a huge part of my life. The difference is I am an adult now and more mature spiritually. I am certain that even though the Lord will more than likely call one of us home before the other, we will only be separated for a time, because I know I will spend eternity with my precious mother. Now my "worry triggers" tend to lean toward my children and grandchildren. They still have a lot of life to live, and I long for their lives to be well spent.

Who or what do you worry about?

_____

_____

Write Matthew 11:28:

_____

_____

Worry burdens me and makes me weary. What about you? So, what do we do? Well, we go to Jesus. Yes, of course! We go to Him and lay down our worry at the foot of the cross, get up, walk away, and we are good to go. Not me! Sorry, it sounds good, but I have failed at this too many times. I walk away, then turn right back around and pick it up again. You too?

Dear sister, there is a way to have peace instead of worry. Grab a highlighter and turn to Philippians 4:6–7 in your Bible. Highlight it, then write it, and let it soak into your soul. I pray that it will be a revelation to you.

_____

_____

Do you want to conquer worry? Then here's what you are to do.
1. Bring your requests and petitions (all those worries) to the Lord.
2. Bring also your thanksgiving.
3. Make it all known to Him.

When you do this, what is the outcome?

_____

_____

Please hear me. The Word of God says that peace that you can't begin to explain will replace that knot in the pit of your stomach when you bring everything to the Lord **with thanksgiving**. I believe the "with thanksgiving" is so often what we leave out.

Let's give this a whirl:

Oh Lord, I am concerned. No, I am worried, anxious, Lord, about

_____

_____

It is more than I can carry. Lord, You have said that when I am weary, You want me to come to You. You have told me to bring all my requests and petitions to You. Lord, I am bringing my worries to You now. Lord, I know that You love me, and I am so thankful for that! I know that You only want what is best for me. Lord, You are God Almighty who is worthy of my praise! There is nothing too hard for You, Lord. I am so thankful that You are my God and that You can do all things. I give these worries to You, Lord, knowing that You will work all things for the good of those who love You, and who have been called according to Your purpose. I praise You for who You are and what You are going to do in this circumstance. I trust You, Lord.

A few years ago I was walking on our college campus with praise music on my iPod. While listening, God answered a prayer for me that I had prayed a few days before. I had told the Lord that I felt my prayer life was in a dry season, and I needed guidance from Him on what I needed to do. So there I was, praise music pouring into my ears, but bursting out in my soul! I thought I was going to explode with thanksgiving to my great God. Peace dissipated the negative, anxious thoughts that had me all tied up prior to that moment. In my spirit, God impressed these words in me as if He was leaning into me, whispering them: "Your prayers are missing praise, the thanksgiving of the heart."

Are your prayers missing praise? _____

Worry and anxiety can't cohabit with peace. Peace will supersede them every time.

**When it snows, she has no fear for her house-
hold; for all of them are clothed in scarlet.
(Proverbs 31:21)**

Wrap Up: Our virtuous woman has learned to lean on the provision of her Father. Without fear or worry, she does what she can do, then she trusts in the promises of God.

One more thing! Their garments were made with a red material (scarlet) that retained the heat. These clothes were probably even doubled in texture and warmth. Our Proverbs 31 woman did what she could for her household, but, ultimately, was secure in knowing her Provider would watch over and care for them. God's provision is always the best, dear sister. Don't worry about your life, He's providing!

Close in prayer. Don't forget the praise! It will be pleasing to Him because it's the thanksgiving of your heart toward your Father who loves you so much.

Endnotes:
[1]The Times of Israel/www.timesofisrael.com, By Times of Israel staff/December 13,2013, 1:41pm/Updated: December 13, 2013, 4:20pm https://www.timesofisrael.com/jerusalem-braces-for-storm-three-times-worse-than-what-has-been-seen-so-far/
[2]WebMD, www.webmd.com/balance/guide/how-worry-affects-your-body/
[3]Ibid.

She Is Provider and Manager

I n our last lesson we focused on worry. We all, at least on occasion, struggle with worry and anxiousness. We explored the effects of excessive worry on our bodies. Before we ended our lesson, we saw in Scripture how to overcome worry and anxiety in our lives.

Write Philippians 4:6–7.

Our godly Proverbs 31 woman didn't let worry get the best of her. She was an overcomer! She provided and managed her household as God led her, and she trusted Him through the process.

KJV	NASB	NIV
She maketh herself coverings of tapestry; her clothing is silk and purple.	She makes coverings for herself; her clothing is fine linen and purple.	She makes coverings for her bed; she is clothed in fine linen and purple.

Read Ruth 2:1–12 as a review.

Ruth, our example of a woman of noble character was trusting. Let's note a couple of things:

1. She continued in what she started.
2. She trusted those around her.

Keeping those two things in mind, read verses 13–16 below. As you do, remember Ruth's posture before Boaz. She was bowed down with her face to the ground.

> "May I continue to find favor in your eyes, my lord," she said. "You have given me comfort and have spoken kindly to your servant—though I do not have the standing of one of your servant girls." (Ruth 2:13)

> At mealtime, Boaz said to her, "Come over here. Have some bread and dip it in the wine vinegar." When she sat down with the harvesters, he offered her some roasted grain. She ate all she wanted and had some left over. As she got up to glean, Boaz gave orders to his men, "Even if she gathers among the sheaves, don't embarrass her. Rather, pull out some stalks for her from the bundles and leave them for her to pick up, and don't rebuke her." (Ruth 2:14–16)

Ruth knew she was being showed favor. There's a time lapse between verses 13 and 14. After verse 13, Ruth returned to her work. I wonder how long Boaz watched her. He might have moved on and came back at mealtime. Somehow, I believe he didn't go far away from this woman who had his full attention.

Let's assume he stayed at this field and kept a watchful eye on Ruth.

What might have been some things he noticed about her?

_____

_____

Look back at verses 11 and 12. How might watching her now confirm to him what he had been told about her?

_____

_____

I have just had a holy highlighted moment! God has high-lighted the phase "you have given me comfort" in my spirit. We have to consider how Ruth must have been feeling as she made her steps to his field. Obviously, she needed comforting since she recognized that Boaz was providing that for her.

Go ahead, put yourself in Ruth's sandals. How might she have been feeling as she arrived at Boaz's field, and continued to feel as she worked that morning?

_____

_____

This is a reminder for me that the will of God is not always a comfortable place. But God will send comforters along the way just like He did for Ruth. There will be Boazes in our lives. God will make sure of it!

The sound of "it's time to eat" must have been a welcoming sound for all the harvesters. It meant a time of rest and refueling. For Ruth, it became more than that.

What happened (v. 14)?

_____

_____

How did Ruth trust Boaz? Before answering, consider all that we have learned about her past and present. Here's some to consider, but add to my list if something comes to your mind: all the loss in her life, being a foreigner, new to Bethlehem, trying to acclimate herself to a new culture and new responsibilities, and feeling inadequate and uncomfortable. Again, how did Ruth trust Boaz?

_____

_____

She ate all she wanted and had some left over. Read Ruth 2:15 in your Bible.

After lunch, Ruth got up and went back to her work gleaning. Ruth was unaware of it at the time, but Boaz continued to take care of her.

Now read verses 17 and 18. Follow my lead and record what happened.
1. Ruth gleaned in the field until evening.
2. She threshed the barley she gathered.
3. She carried _____

4. Ruth also brought out and gave_____

In what ways did Ruth provide?

_____

_____

How had she managed her day?

_____

_____

Ruth worked hard managing her time so that she could provide for herself and Naomi. In Proverbs 31:22, our wife and mother managed her home to provide for her family. She didn't worry about the snow (Proverbs 31:21) because she had done her part in managing and providing. She trusted in God's will for her life, though uncomfortable at times; she could rest because of whom she was trusting in.

> Trust in the LORD with all your heart and lean not on your own understanding; in all your ways acknowledge him, and he will make your paths straight. (Proverbs 3:5–6)

Write Psalm 37:3.

_____

_____

How does this verse apply to Ruth, and what we have learned today?

_____

_____

Our Proverbs 31 woman was clothed in fine linen and purple. Fine linen would have been a valuable and desirable commodity. Spiritually speaking, she was clothed in the finest because she dwelt in the land of trust; therefore, she enjoyed safe pasture.

Trusting God has its payoff. Close today by reading Psalm 23 out loud.

> **She makes coverings for her bed; she is clothed
> in fine linen and purple. (Proverbs 31:22)**

Wrap Up: Our virtuous woman knows how to provide and manage her household, always relying on God for His guidance and also others as God directs.

She Is Humble

PROVERBS 31:23

I hope that you are seeing that it's not about what we do. It's about who we are, because of whose we are. That is what drives what we do.

Has God called us to be doers? Yes, of course! Jesus was a doer! But our act of doing is driven by trust, love, commitment, submission, compassion, kindness, generosity ... all that made our godly woman who she was, as well as the virtuous woman of today.

KJV	NASB	NIV
Her husband is known in the gates, when he sitteth among the elders of the land.	Her husband is known in the gates, when he sits among the elders of the land.	Her husband is respected at the city gate, where he takes his seat among the elders of the land.

The last verse that her husband was mentioned in was in Proverbs 31:11: "Her husband has full confidence in her."

Our verse in this lesson appears to be about her husband in the midst of verses about her; therefore, it appears to me that her husband is respected here because of her.

In what ways can a person gain respect because of another? I'm thinking of a few different scenarios.

Think about an employer and an employee(s). How can an employee's work gain respect for the employer?

_____

_____

Now, what about between friends? One friend is respected among their peers because of another friend. How?

_____

_____

I am trying to help you consider how our Proverbs 31 woman could have brought her husband respect at the city gate.

Any thoughts?

_____

_____

A boss at a workplace will be praised and maybe even promoted because of his team's work; a circle of friends works on a community project together, all working equally hard, but only one is praised and given all the credit; a wife uses her gifts and talents and helps her husband with his responsibilities in an organization he is a part of, and he is honored for his work. The employee, friend, and wife take a step back to let others shine.

All of this is because of humility. Our Proverbs 31 woman was humble. Humble people focus more on God and others than they do on themselves. They don't have to orchestrate attention for themselves because they understand that as they focus on God and others, God Himself will give them moments of fame. But here's the thing, truly humble people aren't waiting or even expecting those moments. Yet God will lift them up as He chooses, just as He did for Ruth.

> God mocks proud mockers but gives grace to the humble. (Proverbs 3:34)

> Humble yourselves before the Lord, and he will lift you up. (James 4:10)

A wife can certainly bring respect to her husband by reaching out to others in kindness. The kindness and willingness to help others will be talked about, I assure you. I think about how Boaz had heard about all that Ruth had done. That wasn't hearsay or speculation. It came right out of the mouth of Naomi. Remember when the women rallied around Naomi when she arrived back in Bethlehem? Well ... that was only the beginning of telling all who would listen about the prize that came back with her, her beloved Ruth.

Let's see the humility of Ruth in the pages of Scripture.

But first, there is a term that you may not be familiar with: *kinsman-redeemer.* If a man died without a son (Ruth's husband) to inherit his possessions, then his closest living male relative was to marry his widow as a kinsman-redeemer, and their first-born son became the heir of the deceased man. We will revisit this a little later.

Read Ruth 2:18–23.

How do you see humility in Ruth?

_____

_____

There are misconceptions about humility, I fear. This "poor me" mentality is not humility, because the focus is on self. Remember, humble people focus on God and others first.

A few years ago, I was going through "a season," if you know what I mean. It was a hard time, but even though the events of the season had passed, I was still holding on for dear life and feeling sorry for myself BIG TIME! God was so patient with me. He certainly endured long suffering as I remained in a pitiful state of being. This went on for weeks. One morning, after a time of talking to God again about the whys and the hows of my past crisis, I moved on to ask God to make me more like Jesus. That's when it hit me. There is nothing pitiful about Jesus! I felt like God dropped that in me in a split second of time. I got down on my face in a field, and right then and there, I repented.

How hard is humility for you?

_____

_____

Do you ever find yourself in this place? "Hey! I did that! I deserve the compliments! I deserve the raise!" Don't you worry your sweet little head about it. God knows who did the work. God knows who made the sacrifices. He knows! Keep your eyes on the One who knows. In due time, He will lift you up. In the meantime, you have a great cloud of witnesses cheering you on as you walk out this life's journey.

About twenty years ago at Christmas, my mother and sisters set up a dream come true for me. I'll start by giving you a little background. I was a part of the award-winning 1977 National Champions, the Murray High School Marching Band. My high school years were centered on this band program that I loved so much. There were lots of fun times, but the most exuberating time for me was home football games. No, it wasn't the halftime show! It was the victory line that we formed before the game started. My heart is racing right now as I relive it in my mind. You think I'm joking, but I'm not. As the cheerleaders and the band made our way onto the field to wait for the team to burst through the paper and run through the line, I would feel like I would explode with excitement.

At some point, I had shared a dream of mine about running through a line of supporters just like the football team. You probably know right now where I found myself one beautiful night with my family and extended family of grandparents, aunts, uncles, and cousins. After we enjoyed the traditional Christmas celebration, my mother announced to the house full of people that we were going to make a dream come true. My sisters helped her organize the crowd to make a victory line. The line extended from out in the yard right up to the front door. I ran through the line in between two rows of family members giving me high fives as they cheered me on. I can still hear the glorious sounds of that night. I ran through the opening of the front door into the house, turned around, and ran back through the line again. I continued this about three times until my family decided enough was enough.

Write Hebrews 12:1.

_____

_____

The saints, "all commended for their faith" (Hebrews 11:39), are cheering you on right now as you run your life's race. Enjoy the victory line!

Her husband is respected at the city gate, where he takes his seat among the elders of the land. (Proverbs 31:23)

Wrap Up: Our virtuous woman is a woman of humility. Her focus is on God and others. She realizes running the good race of faith will only be accomplished by fixing her eyes on Jesus, the Author and Perfecter of her faith.

How has God spoken to you today?

_____

_____

End this lesson by thanking Him for what He has revealed to you.

She Is Respected

PROVERBS 31:24

In our last lesson we saw that our Proverbs 31 woman humbly lived in such a way that it brought attention and respect to her husband among his peers.

Today, we will see that she was also respected.

KJV	NASB	NIV
She maketh fine linen, and selleth it; and delivereth girdles unto the merchants.	She makes linen garments and sells them, and supplies belts to the tradesmen.	She makes linen garments and sells them, and supplies the merchants with sashes.

God is teaching me so much in this study. In the past when I would read through Proverbs 31, at this point, I would be deflated. "How can any woman live up to this one?" I would think to myself.

I am literally praying right now that God is clearing up for both of us that His Proverbs 31 woman is who He is currently making us to be. He is! If you are surrendered to His will for your life, you are one step closer today than you were yesterday. I hope that is encouragement for you to keep going.

In today's lesson, we will learn even more about the extent of the respect that Boaz had for Ruth. But first, I want us to look at Boaz. He was the son of Rahab. Heard of her? This Rahab may have been the one we read about in Joshua. Turn in your Bible to Joshua 2:1.

Who was Rahab? _____

Now finish reading chapter 2 of Joshua.

If Boaz's mother was the Rahab of Joshua, what would be some of the things she might have taught her son about the Lord?

_____

_____

I realize she might have been sensitive in sharing certain things about her life. But, I can only imagine from her past career as a prostitute what her perspectives were about hope for a new life and about God's grace and mercy.

Let's have some fun and try to imagine a time of sharing she might have had with her boy (Boaz).

"At the time of hiding those spies, I didn't understand what compelled me to do what I did. But it wasn't long until I realized it wasn't what, but who was compelling me. When I went up to that rooftop to talk to those men, God gave me such confidence and peace. I made them swear that they would show kindness to our family by saving us from death because I was showing kindness to them. When I think about it now, that was a very dangerous thing I did, but it was part of God's plan. It is so evident to see now when I look back. Why in the world did God choose me? I have been able to live my life since unashamed, somehow, of my past. It's weird, I know! Even to me. All I can say is, feeling His forgiveness over me changed me. His unimaginable grace and mercy is beyond any words I might have. Son, He takes us as we are, past and all, and offers us life."

Knowing Boaz's roots helps me better understand why Ruth's past as a Moabitess, a foreigner who worshipped false gods, would not have been a stumbling block for him.

Read Ruth 3:1–14.

The harvest is now past. The reaping of the barley and wheat was completed. It was brought to the threshing floor. The threshing floor was "a flat surface prepared for the threshing of grain. The threshing floor was usually located at the edge of a village, frequently on a large flat rock outcropping. When no flat rock was available, the threshing floor would be prepared by leveling the ground and pounding the earth to create a hard surface." Here in the threshing floor, winnowing would take place. Winnowing is "the process of separating the kernels of grain, such as wheat or barley, from the chaff with a current of air. The grain and its mixture of straw and husks were thrown into the air. The kernels of wheat or barley would fall into a pile on the threshing floor; the chaff, or refuse, would be blown away by the wind."[1]

From what is recorded, Boaz had only seen Ruth dirty and sweaty. Until now, that is. Naomi's instructions to Ruth: "Get cleaned up! Put on the prettiest dress you have. That blue one with the lacey trim would be nice." (Okay, I added some of my own words!)

The celebration of the Feast of Firstfruits would be taking place at this time. Naomi instructed Ruth to wait until the festivities were done. Boaz would have laid down beside his pile of grain to protect it from thieves. Ruth followed her mother-in-law's instructions, which were, "When he lies down, note the place where he is lying. Then go and uncover his feet and lie down. He will tell you what to do."

> In the middle of the night something startled the man, and he turned and discovered a woman lying at this feet.
> "Who are you?" he asked.
> "I am your servant Ruth," she said. "Spread the corner of your garment over me, since you are a kinsman-redeemer." (Ruth 3:8–9)

Basically, Ruth was bold and courageous by taking the initiative to ask Boaz to marry her. Ruth was in need of a redeemer.

Read Boaz's response in Ruth 3:10–18.

Name some of the ways Boaz showed respect for Ruth.

_____

_____

Look closely at Ruth 3:11: "All my fellow townsmen know that you are a [virtuous] woman of noble character."

Who was making her virtuous?_____
How? (Hint: past to present)

_____

_____

Just like Rahab, Ruth had a past. Yet she persevered. She didn't let anything from her past keep her from her future. She showed respect, and she was respected by others, all Boaz's "fellow townsmen."

As far as our Proverbs 31 woman, who made the linen garments and sold them and supplied the merchants with sashes, what I want you to see is how she was respected. She was sought out for what she had to give.

She makes linen garments and sells them, and supplies the merchants with sashes. (Proverbs 31:24)

Wrap Up: Our virtuous woman not only brings her husband respect among his peers, but she is highly respected as well. She lives her life in such a way that others notice her and admire the choices she makes.

If you are struggling with your past, God says you missed the new mercies you woke up to this morning.

> Because of the LORD's great love we are not consumed, for his compassions [mercies] never fail. They are new every morning; great is your faithfulness. (Lamentations 3:22-23)

Close with prayer.

Endnotes:
[1] *Nelson's New Illustrated Bible Dictionary*, ed. Ronald F. Young-blood (Nashville: Thomas Nelson, 1995).

Royal Reflection

One of the saddest places I have ever been was on the grounds of the former Nazi camp, Auschwitz. "It was the largest Nazi concentration camp for prisoners of various nationalities and the largest mass extermination center of European Jews".[1]

Although today the grounds, buildings, and collections are all part of the State Museum Auschwitz-Birkenau, oppression lurks over that place like a morning fog.

For me, it is difficult to understand why such a place had to exist at all! The fact that so many innocent people, men, women and children, suffered and died there is heartbreaking.

One of the exhibits caused the tears in my eyes to spill over down my cheeks. Beyond the glass that I looked through was a space of nothing but suitcases stacked one upon another. You see, the people packed their suitcases because they were going to a better place, or so they thought. The spirit of deception hung over those suitcases as I stood there stunned by what I saw on them, not names but numbers. The prisoners were known by their numbers. The sight of this cause me more anguish than I can even express.

It was at that moment the Lord impressed on me so strongly that I flinched, "They were not a number to Me; I knew every one of their names."

Evil saturated in deception is tormenting our society. Satan and his demonic forces would love nothing more than the lost to remain lost and the saved, those freed in Christ, to live as slaves to bondage. Think about it. If we are weighed down in bondage, we become enslaved to anxiety, fear, and weariness, destroying our witness.

You are free in Christ. There's nothing holding you back from what lies ahead for you. You are part of His royal family. Don't believe the deception of the enemy. Believe God at His Word! The promises He has made, He will keep!

Endnotes:
[1] Screenplay written and directed by Krzysztof Miklaszewski Auschwitz History-Present-future, copyright The Auschwitz-birkenau State Musuem, 1994

She Is Confident

PROVERBS 31:25

I have never been one who likes to get my hair wet. Swimming pools are great, but don't splash me, please, because the water may hit my hair. I have spent many hours fully clothed at pools watching my grandchildren play. So many times I have watched people walk in, lay their towel down, walk straight to the diving board and dive into the water headfirst. Can you believe these people choose to get their hair wet first thing? Well, dear sister, that's what we are going to do today! We're going to dive in headfirst into God's Word. Wait! Let me put on a shower cap. Okay. I'm ready! Ready, set, go!

> Now faith is being sure of what we hope for and certain of what we do not see. (Hebrews 11:1)

> And without faith it is impossible to please God, because anyone who comes to him must believe that he exists and that he rewards those who earnestly seek him. (Hebrews 11:6)

Our Proverbs 31 woman lived by faith.

KJV	NASB	NIV
Strength and honour are her clothing; and she shall rejoice in time to come.	Strength and dignity are her clothing, and she smiles at the future.	She is clothed with strength and dignity; she can laugh at the days to come.

Every Proverbs 31 woman is clothed with strength and dignity. After studying different resources on the meaning of these two words, I think I'm ready to give you a mental picture of the virtuous woman who is wearing strength and dignity.

Look at the woman who just walked in the room. There's something different about her. She's confident, yes, but not in an 'I have it all together' kind of way. I have heard about what she has been going through, yet she looks so strong. I see a stubborn strength in her, which is only a part of her beauty. She's certainly attractive enough, but there's something about her that's unique. I ran into her at a paint store one Saturday morning a few months ago. Outwardly, one would say she was a mess. No make-up, dressed in old paint-splattered oversized clothes, and her hair looked like she had just rolled out of bed. We stood there, both waiting for our paint to be mixed and engaged in a little conversation. Her paint was ready first, we said our goodbyes, and as I watched her leave the store, I remember thinking to myself how beautiful she was. Maybe what I saw in her was a splendor in her countenance, a holy confidence.

Nothing can match the holy confidence resulting from faith. In a future lesson we will talk about outward beauty, but for now, may I say I wouldn't trade the inward beauty of a life lived in faith for anything.

Faith causes us to endure. Why? Because by faith we believe God exists and that He formed the universe by His command.

We believe that He is greater than all of our problems. We believe that He is able and willing to help us and deliver us from the evil forces—and even from our own evil desires. We believe that He loved mankind so much that He sent His only Son to die in our place so that we have the glorious freedom from sin and eternal life. We believe that no matter how bleak our life looks at times that He is sovereign, which means nothing is out of His control. And we believe all of this without physically seeing Him. That is faith, dear sibling.

I'm thinking of Ruth right now. She had her faith tested, didn't she? Remember that she proposed marriage to Boaz in chapter 3. But there was a hiccup in the plan, although Boaz was certainly in favor of the marriage. There was another relative standing in the way.

Read Ruth 3:18 in your Bible.

What was Naomi's instruction to Ruth?

_____

_____

Wait? Are you kidding me? We don't like to wait, do we? I see no evidence of Ruth wringing her hands. I do see from Ruth 3:13 that Boaz was firmly rooted in faith.

> Stay here for the night, and in the morning if he wants to redeem, good; let him redeem. But if he is not willing, as surely as the LORD lives I will do it. Lie here until morning. (Ruth 3:13)

I believe that Ruth and Boaz together stood firm in faith, believing God's plan would indeed come to pass, and however it looked, they would accept it.

We have spent so much time dissecting the Proverbs 31 woman using Ruth as our biblical example. We have confirmed over and over how much Ruth trusted God. But there's no trust without faith.

One day, while driving in our car, I asked the Lord to give me a visual on faith versus trust. They always seem to go hand in hand. Well, the Lord answered that prayer for me within a couple of minutes, literally! He used a flock of birds to teach me. As He directed me to notice the birds overhead, my eyes locked on one little bird in particular. He was flapping his wings as if to say, "I believe, I believe." God impressed on me, "That's faith. It takes work on your part." As I continued to watch the little bird, his wings soon spread out and he soared with such gracefulness. God said, "That's trust." Trust is part of the process when we rest in our Lord with confidence in His ability and His character, knowing that He is in control. That little bird would flap his wings, then soar, flap his wings, then soar as he moved across the sky. God said, "That's Christian growth."

The faith/trust process is part of the much bigger process of believing God, believing that He will actually do what He has promised.

In Hebrews 11 we see a list of those who were commended for their faith. What did each one do by faith?

By faith Abel

By faith Enoch

By faith Noah

By faith Abraham

By faith Isaac

By faith Jacob

By faith Joseph

By faith Moses

By faith the people

By faith the walls of Jericho

By faith the prostitute Rahab (Boaz's mom)

Finish reading Hebrews 11:32–40.

By faith kingdoms are conquered, lions' mouths are shut, the dead are brought back to life....

By faith Ruth accompanied Naomi to Bethlehem. She trusted God, and He commended her for her faith.

The Proverbs 31 woman who was clothed in strength and dignity laughed at the days to come because she had faith that the One who was holding her would take care of her. She faced the future with confidence, choosing to rejoice with gladness.

She is clothed with strength and dignity; she can laugh at the days to come. (Proverbs 31:25)

Wrap Up: Our virtuous woman is a woman of confidence. Her dependency on the Lord continues to increase as she walks with Him in faith. The confidence she possesses is not in her ability but is His in her.

What are you currently facing that requires you to walk in faith?

_____

_____

Close today by asking God to help you see the faith within you.

She Is Wise

T his is what a Bible study from the Middletown Bible
Church has to say about this Proverbs 31 verse:

This is the only verse in this passage which
speaks of the godly woman's tongue and the
words of her mouth. Our Lord taught that "out
of the overflow of the heart the mouth speaks"
(Matthew 12:34). What comes out of the mouth
is an indication of what is in the heart. Our
speech reveals our heart. Out of a wise heart
come wise words. Out of a kind heart come kind
words. Out of a loving heart come loving words.[1]

KJV	NASB	NIV
She openeth her mouth with wisdom; and in her tongue is the law of kindness.	She opens her mouth in wisdom, and the teaching of kindness is on her tongue.	She speaks with wisdom, and faithful instruction is on her tongue.

The Hebrew word *chokmah* for wisdom can refer to technical skills or special abilities in fashioning something.[2] *Chokmah*

appears in the following verse when the Lord was speaking to Moses:

> Tell all the skilled men to whom I have given wisdom in such matters that they are to make garments for Aaron, for his consecration, so he may serve me as priest. (Exodus 28:3)

Chokmah also means "the knowledge and the ability to make the right choices at the opportune time."[2] Wisdom is knowledge with understanding, and it's from the Lord.

While Naomi and Ruth were talking about what had happened the night before with Boaz, Boaz was at the city gate.

The legal provision required a dead man's brother to marry his childless widow and father a son who would assume the dead man's name and inherit his portion of the Promised Land (Deuteronomy 25:5–10). The practice is an important element in the story of Ruth. In Ruth's case, her brother-in-law had also died. So Boaz was at the city gate waiting for the man who was a relative (kinsman-redeemer) nearer than himself.

The city (town) gate was a busy place. No one could leave or enter town without going through the gate. Merchants were set up there to trade and/or sell their products. Because of all the people there, it was the place to find witnesses. Boaz sat down and waited.

Sometimes wisdom is exhibited by staying back. And that's exactly what our Ruth was doing! Let's focus in on wise Boaz.

Meanwhile Boaz went up to the town gate and sat there. When the kinsman-redeemer he had mentioned came along, Boaz said, "Come over here, my friend, and sit down. So he went over and sat down. Boaz took ten of the elders of the town and said, "Sit here," and they did so. Then he said to the kinsman-redeemer, "Naomi, who has come back from Moab, is selling the piece of land that belonged to our brother Elimelech. I thought I should bring the matter to your attention and suggest that you buy it in the presence of the elders of my people. If you will redeem it, do so. But if you will not, tell me, so I will know. For no one has the right to do it except you, and I am next in line."

"I will redeem it," he said.

Then Boaz said, "On the day you buy the land from Naomi and from Ruth the Moabitess, you acquire the dead man's widow, in order to maintain the name of the dead with his property."

(Ruth 4:1–5)

List the ways Boaz used wisdom here. Go back and review the meanings of wisdom on the previous page if you need to.

_____

_____

Boaz was a businessman. He had the "technical skills" and "special abilities" to work out this matter.

A few things you might have noted: We don't know how long Boaz waited, but he waited. Boaz took ten of the town's elders with him as witnesses. The order in which he laid out the matter demonstrates great wisdom. Notice how and when he mentioned Ruth. He also made sure he mentioned that she was from Moab.

Why would this have made a difference?

_____

_____

To redeem, not only must a kinsman-redeemer be a member of the family in trouble, but he must also have the means to pay the debt of redemption. Most of the time, those who were in need of redemption were poor people who had lost everything they possessed. They could not redeem themselves but needed the help of a redeemer who possessed enough resources to pay their debt.

The nearer kinsman-redeemer was ready to redeem until the part about acquiring the dead man's widow came up.

> At this, the kinsman-redeemer said, "Then I can-
> not redeem it because I might endanger my own
> estate. You redeem it yourself. I cannot do it."
> (Ruth 4:6)

The man didn't want to complicate his inheritance. Who could blame him! If he had a son through Ruth, some of his estate would transfer away from his family to the family of Elimelech. It seemed that Boaz had some idea that this might be the case. He laid it out as such. He had knowledge and the ability to make the right choices at the opportune time.

(Now in earlier times in Israel, for the redemption and transfer of property to become final, one party took off his sandal and gave it to the other. This was the method of legalizing transactions in Israel.) So the kinsman-redeemer said to Boaz, "Buy it yourself." And he removed his sandal. (Ruth 4:7–8)

These verses were holy highlighted for me; therefore, I did some digging, and this was what I learned:

It had been a custom in Israel that when a man bought property, the seller gave the buyer his shoes. The new owner would put on the shoes of the former land owner and then walk all around the borders of his new property.

Write Mark 1:7.

Hundreds of years later, John the Baptist might have remembered this custom when he said, "the thongs of whose sandals I am not worthy to stoop down and untie."

The kingdom of God did not belong to John the Baptist, although people were treating him like it did. It was as if John the Baptist was saying, "Listen, I'm not the owner. But I know the Owner, and I am not even worthy to stoop down and untie his sandals."

His name is Jesus, and He gives wisdom.

Before we conclude our lesson, let's take a look at the wisest king who ever lived.

Read 1 Kings 4:29–34.
How much wisdom did the Lord give Solomon?

How many proverbs did he speak?

And his songs numbered?

> Men of all nations came to listen to Solomon's wisdom, sent by all the kings of the world, who had heard of his wisdom. (1 Kings 4:34)

Solomon became king after his father, David.

Turn back in your Bible to 1 Kings 3 and read verses 1–5.

Can you imagine the God of the universe appearing to you and saying, "Ask for whatever you want me to give you"?

Solomon answered God by saying: Read 1 Kings 3:6–10.

How did the Lord respond to Solomon's answer? (vv. 11–14)

―――――――――――――――――――――――――――――――――――――――

―――――――――――――――――――――――――――――――――――――――

We know from 1 Kings 4:29–34 that God did exactly what He told Solomon He would do. It was reconfirmed in 1 Kings 5:12: "The Lord gave Solomon wisdom, just as he had promised him."

What did Solomon have to do to receive great wisdom?

That's right, with a desiring heart that only wanted to please the Lord, he asked for wisdom.

Write James 1:5.

_____

_____

**She speaks with wisdom, and faithful instruction
is on her tongue. (Proverbs 31:26)**

Wrap Up: Our virtuous woman is a woman who has the desire in her heart to discern between right and wrong, good and evil. She has responsibilities and so many are depending on her. She doesn't seek self-help guides for her answers. She asks for wisdom from the only One who can give it.

Do you desire wisdom? Do you desire to have faithful instruction on your tongue? We all need wisdom. Ask Him; don't delay in receiving what only He can give.

Lord, give me a discerning heart to

_____

_____

Endnotes:
[1]Middletown Bible Church, "Christian Home and Family: The Virtuous Woman of Proverbs 31," http://www.middletownbiblechurch.org/homefam/pr31text.pdf
[2]James Strong, *The New Strong's Expanded Exhaustive Concordance of the Bible* (Nashville: Thomas Nelson, 2010).

She Is Watchful

In Tiffany's teenage years I proved to her over and over that I had knowledge of things she didn't necessarily want me to know. If asked, Tiffany would probably confirm that she would have believed that her mother had eyes in the back of her head! (And, I would say, "Had? No baby, still have!") You know what I'm talking about. Antennas up when something's not as it should be, not to mention the "momma senses" on high alert. Tiffany would also tell a teenager today, "Don't think you're hiding because you will turn around and there she will be, as if she just appeared from ... somewhere."

We have been equipped with the radar, Sister! Our Proverbs 31 woman was no different. She made her family her business, antennas up and "momma senses" on high alert!

KJV	NASB	NIV
She looketh well to the ways of her household and eateth not the bread of idleness.	She looks well to the ways of her household, and does not eat the bread of idleness.	She watches over the affairs of her household and does not eat the bread of idleness.

The *Keil and Delitzsch Commentary on the Old Testament* says this:

> She looks how it goes in her house. Her eyes
> are turned everywhere; she is at one time here,
> at another there, to look after all with her own
> eyes; she does not suffer the day's work, accord-
> ing to the instructions given, to be left undone,
> while she folds her own hands on her bosom; but
> she works, keeping an oversight on all sides, and
> does not eat the bread of idleness, but bread well
> deserved.[1]

This would certainly describe Ruth, the betrothed bride of Boaz. But for now, as we look in on Scripture, it's Boaz that we see as watchful.

Read Ruth 4:9–10 in your Bible.

How do you see Boaz as watchful (and cautious)?

Boaz didn't delay in making good on his promise to Ruth. He moved quickly to claim and receive the right of redemption both for Elimelech's land and Ruth.

> By purchasing all of Naomi's property and goods,
> Boaz has undertaken the total care of Naomi and
> the obligation to support her in life and provide
> for her in death. By acquiring Ruth, he has obli-
> gated himself to give her the opportunity to bear
> children, the first of whom would then become
> the heir of Elimelech and his sons. [2]

Orpah had been redeemed as well, yet unknowingly.

Boaz called the elders as witnesses to the transaction as he took possession of Naomi's property and acquired Ruth the Moabitess.

How is Boaz a picture of Jesus Christ in this redemption story?

_____

_____

"Boaz is a beautiful illustration of the Lord Jesus Christ who became mankind's kinsman-redeemer and who makes things right before God, the Father for those who trust in Him."[3] Jesus had the means to pay the debt of redemption. Mankind could not redeem itself. We needed the help of a redeemer who possessed enough resources to pay our debt, who better than God's only Son.

Ray Stedman, one of my favorite teachers of the Word, had this to say:

> The Lord Jesus left his glory in heaven and came to earth as our redeemer to die upon the cross. He brought all the fallen estate of Adam for every inhabitant of the earth, without exception. Every man, woman, and child in this world has been redeemed already by the grace of the Lord Jesus Christ. He has bought back all the fallen estate of the sons of Adam—whoever they might be— Mahlon and Chilion and Elimelech. But where was Orpah in this picture? Ruth was ready to en- ter into all the value of Boaz's activity for her, and

Orpah could have had it too. But because Orpah
turned and went back to her own people and to
her own gods, she is never heard from again –
she has no part in the inheritance. Though Boaz
bought the entire inheritance of her husband as
well as Ruth's, Orpah is lost in this picture because
she turned and went back to her own people and
to her own gods.[4]

Fill in the blanks.
(Mark 10:45) "For even the Son of Man did not come to be
served, but to serve, and to give his life as a _____ for
_____."

(Job 19:25) "I know that my _____ lives, and that in
the end he will stand upon the earth."

Redeemer—one who frees or delivers another from difficulty,
danger, or bondage, usually by the payment of a ransom price.[5]

The perfect Lamb of God went to the cross and paid the ransom price once and for all, covering all sin, completely.

We have been made holy through the sacrifice of
the body of Jesus Christ once for all. (Hebrews
10:10)

In him we have redemption through his blood,
the forgiveness of sins, in accordance with the
riches of God's grace that he lavished on us
with all wisdom and understanding. (Ephesians
1:7–8)

He gave His life, yes, died and was buried, but on that glorious third day, He rose from the grave. Like Job, I proclaim that "I know my Redeemer lives and that in the end He will stand upon the earth."

Ray Stedman's commentary on the Book of Ruth is titled "The Romance of Redemption." Part of my "romance of redemption" story is this: As a little girl I prayed to God every day. I knew Him then as Creator. I reasoned that the God who created the universe could certainly watch out for me. I knew I had a hole within me that couldn't be filled with things of this world. As I grew to a preteen, I couldn't begin to identify, much less understand, the emptiness in me. I was always so desperate for the love of God. I remember so vividly the season of my acceptance of His grace. At the time I didn't know that the tugging within me was the Holy Spirit drawing me, wooing me, to Him. As I resisted the surrender I felt miserable, lonely and restless. I don't remember the length of time I resisted Him, but I remember the day in a church service that I had a choice to make, just like Orpah. I could have looked back and stayed back, but I didn't. As the invitation that day was extended, like Ruth, I sought after the God who loved me. I'm smiling right now as I think about how the Lord might have whispered to our pastor in His still, small voice, "Keep singing. My girl is on her way."

With knees shaking, my grip on the pew in front of me broke loose, and I slipped out and walked the distance down the aisle to our pastor who prayed with me as I accepted new life in Christ. In that moment, I received forgiveness, and my love relationship with my Savior began. He died for mankind, and that day, I recognized by my obedience to His calling that He died for me. I received His grace. My Redeemer became my Savior and the Lord of my life as I committed the rest of my days to His care.

> For the eyes of the LORD range throughout the earth to strengthen those whose hearts are fully committed to him. (2 Chronicles 16:9)

Our Proverbs 31 woman was fully committed to the Lord, and her heart was strengthened by Him.

She watches over the affairs of her household and does not eat the bread of idleness. (Proverbs 31:27)

Wrap Up: Our virtuous woman has a love relationship with God. She is diligent in training up her children in His ways. She keeps a watchful eye on the affairs of her home.

Recall your "romance of redemption" story in part. Our story continues, dear sister. End today by writing the part that God brings to your mind.

Endnotes:

[1]C. F. Keil and F. Delitzsch, *Keil and Delitzsch Commentary on the Old Testament*, New Updated Edition (Peabody, MA: Hendrickson Publishers, 1996).

[2]John H. Walton, Victor H. Matthews, and Mark W. Chavalas, *The IVP Bible Background Commentary: Old Testament* (Downers Grove, IL: InterVarsity Press, 2000).

[3]*The Bible Knowledge Commentary*, eds. John S. Walvoord and Roy B. Zuck (Colorado Springs: David C. Cook, 1983) .

[4]Ray C. Stedman, "Ruth: The Romance of Redemption," RayStedman.org, www.raystedman.org/bible-overview/adventuring/ruth-the-romance-of-redemption.

[5]*The American Heritage Dictionary*, Second College Edition, s.v. "redeemer"

She Is Called Blessed

PROVERBS 31:28

In this lesson I want us to consider our legacies. Here are some questions to consider. What are you teaching others by the life you live? What would family and close friends say about you? What would people remember most about you?

Oatman is preparing to speak at his aunt's funeral tomorrow. The portion of Scripture that he will be referring to includes our verse today. I had already begun writing on this lesson when he told me tonight what he plans to share. The hair stood up on the back of my neck. He will be sharing what he remembered most about his aunt and how she influenced his life by the way she prioritized God and by the way she served His church—in other words, her legacy.

KJV	NASB	NIV
Her children arise up, and call her blessed; her husband also, and he praiseth her.	Her children rise up and bless her; her husband also, and he praises her.	Her children arise and call her blessed; her husband also, and he praises her.

Let's think about this. The people who were with this wife and mother (the Proverbs 31 woman) the most saw her at her best and at her worst, and even then they called her blessed and her husband praised her. How? It would seem to me that her attitude and reactions to what life brought her way were not negative. Her disposition and outlook were noticed and admired by those who knew her best.

I thought it might be fun to look at some epitaphs as we consider legacies today.

According to *The American Heritage Dictionary*, an epitaph is "an inscription on a tombstone in memory of the one buried there."[1] For example:

> An unforgettable person[2]
> Asked for so little, but gave so very much[3]
> Brave in spirit, strong in love[4]
> Generous of heart, constant in faith[5]
> She touched everyone with special love and kindness.[6]
> She appreciated every moment because she knew she might never be able to experience it again.[7]
> She took in all the wonders of life, wrapped them in a colorful package and gave it to us.[8]
> She did more than exist, she lived. She did more than listen, she understood.[9]
> She walked in beauty.[10]
> She served and kept the faith.[11]

If you were to write an epitaph for yourself, what would it be?

_____

_____

Let's look at Scripture. This is how God described the following:

David – a man after [God's] own heart (Acts 13:22).

Noah – a righteous man, blameless among the people of his time, and he walked with God (Genesis 6:9).

Moses – (Numbers 12:3).

_____

_____

Joshua – a man exalted by God so that others would know that God was with him (Joshua 3:7).

Ruth – a woman of noble character (Ruth 3:11).

Job – (Job 1:1).

_____

_____

Daniel – (Daniel 1:17–20).

_____

_____

Elijah – (James 5:16–18).

_____

_____

How would God describe you? Remember, you were made by God and are loved by God. Even before your birth, He began making you into what He created you for: "Before I formed you in the womb I knew you, before you were born I set you apart; I appointed you as a prophet to the nations" (Jeremiah 1:5).

Now, with that in mind, you can answer the question, how would God describe you?

_____

_____

I want us to view the verses from Ruth today from the standpoint of how Boaz and Ruth had and would have influenced the kingdom of God for His glory.

> Then the elders and all those at the gate said,
> "We are witnesses. May the LORD make the
> woman who is coming into your home like Ra-
> chel and Leah, who together built up the house
> of Israel. May you have standing in Ephrathah

and be famous in Bethlehem. Through the off-
spring the LORD gives you by this young woman,
may your family be like that of Perez, whom
Tamar bore to Judah. (Ruth 4:11–12)

You'd better believe that our legacies affect generations to
come. How we choose to live our lives matters, not only to us but
also to our children, our grandchildren, and so on.

The baby boys born to Rachel and Leah were ten of the twelve
tribe leaders of Israel. The blessing over Ruth was that her off-
spring, like Rachel and Leah, would be highly important to Israel
and to God.

For Boaz to have the standing in Ephrathah and fame in Bethlehem certainly came about for him. The Book of Ruth alone is
a testimony to all the generations since who have marveled over
Boaz's character.

For now, let's take a quick peek at Ruth 4:18–22.

Why do you think the family line of Perez is important?

_____

_____

Perez was the firstborn of the twin sons of Judah and Tamar.
Boaz was the seventh generation in Perez's family tree; therefore, he was a descendant of Judah.

Fill in the blanks of each name per generation.

Perez	Nahshon
	Boaz
Amminadab	

Consider what we have learned about Boaz and Ruth and how they had influenced the kingdom of God for His glory. Now, answer these three questions for each one.

What did they teach others by the life they lived?
Boaz

Ruth

What would family and close friends have said about them?
Boaz

Ruth

What do we remember most about them?
Boaz

Ruth

> **Her children arise and call her blessed; her husband also, and he praises her. (Proverbs 31:28)**

Wrap Up: Our virtuous woman lives her life to please God. Out of her obedience to the Lord, she has an influence on the lives of others. She is admired and praised for the woman she has become.

Close by answering these three questions.

What am I teaching others by the life I live?

_____

_____

What would family and close friends say about me?

_____

_____

What would people remember most about me?

_____

_____

Pray over your answers. In what areas of your life do you need God's help? Ask Him to help you. Dear sibling, remember we are all a work in progress. If you are feeling discouraged, that is the voice of the enemy. Learn to recognize his condemnation. "There is no condemnation for those who are in Christ Jesus" Romans 8:1.

Endnotes:

[1] *The American Heritage Dictionary*, 2nd College Edition, s.v., "epitaph."

[2] Jason Ropchan, "50 Short Epitaph Examples," Your Tribute, www.resources.yourtribute.com/monuments/epitaph-examples/.

[3] Ibid.

[4] Ibid.

[5] "What Is an Epitaph?" HonorLife, www.headstonesandmemorials.com/Epitaphs_Epitaph_Examples.php.

[6] Ibid.

[7] "Epitaphs for Females—Mother, Daughter, Sister," Everlife Memorials, www.everlifememorials.com/v/headstones/epitaphs-females.htm.

[8] Ibid.

[9] Ibid.

[10] Ibid.

[11] Ibid.

She Is a Blessing

PROVERBS 31:29

In our last lesson, I asked some tough questions. I can assure you before they went down on paper they were asked of me.

Please hear me. I have spent way too many years in defeat. I have given ear to the voice of our enemy too many times to count. Just in the past two weeks I have been literally tormented by him. He has bombarded me with his lies that, sadly, I received, making me feel like a total failure. I believe you can relate when I say the enemy has worn me out and worn me down. Chaos and negativity have tried to consume me. The closer I have gotten to completing this study, the more he's turned up the heat. But ... God. Through the struggle, God's grace has reached out for me and has once again pulled me up to stand firm on the solid foundation of Christ.

Is the chaos still present? Yep. Are the lies still flooding in? Yep. Are negative people still wearing me out? Most definitely! But, I'm praising my God because "the one who is in [me] is greater than the one who is in the world" (1 John 4:4).

Dear sister, do you know what God is doing in you? Do you?

KJV	NASB	NIV
Many daughters have done virtuously, but thou excellest them all.	Many daughters have done nobly, but you excel them all.	Many women do noble things, but you surpass them all.

Think about the women at church, work, organizations you are involved with, members of your family, and your circle of friends.

Name three women that stand out in a positive way among all the others.

1. _____ 2. _____ 3. _____

For each of the women you listed, explain why each one stands out. Then look back at Proverbs 31:11–27 and write the verse number(s) that you attribute to each woman.

Verses for #1:

Verses for #2:

Verses for #3:

Here is another way to view today's verse: There are lots of women, probably too numerous to count, that do good, worthy, even godly deeds, but you go beyond, standing out among them all.

Look at Ruth chapter 4, and read the rest of the chapter starting at verse 13 in your Bible.

The wedding day arrived for Boaz and Ruth. In one verse (13), they married, got pregnant, and gave birth to a son. I don't know about you, but I want to know about the life that was lived out between those major events. But God didn't give us details, did He? In this family of now four, there might have been days where there was one too many. Trying days are part of all our lives, no matter the family dynamics. Mother-in-law Naomi might have been easy to love for Boaz or not. Either way, he had taken her into his family. We certainly know that for Ruth it was a no-brainer! She proved over and over that her love for and commitment to Naomi was steadfast.

Fill in the blank for verse 14.
The women said to Naomi: "Praise be to the _____, who this day has not left you without a kinsman-redeemer. May he become famous throughout Israel."

This verse warms my heart. The women, along with Naomi, were giving credit where credit was due. The Lord was (and is) the Faithful One. He is worthy of all praise and honor.

Naomi's kinsman-redeemer was given a blessing by the women that he would be famous throughout Israel. These women of Israel had no idea how this blessing would play out. They also said that through this child, Naomi's life would be renewed and that he would sustain her in her old age.

> For your daughter-in-law, who loves you and
> who is better to you than seven sons, has given
> him birth."(Ruth 4:15)

264 • KATHY FARLEY

Once again we see recognition for Ruth. Not only for giving birth to the son, but for _____

Sons were important among Jewish people. To have sons was actually a sign of the favor of God upon them. Notice the comparison the women gave in how Ruth loved and cared for Naomi. Ruth was better to her than seven sons would have been.

Feel with me the overwhelming joy in verse 16: "Then Naomi took the child, laid him in her lap and cared for him."

God had not forgotten His Naomi. She had lost so much, but this verse reveals what God had planned all along for her, a grandson to care for. His name was Obed, which means worship. I love how Scripture says "they named him." Oh, how I wish the dialog had been recorded.

In biblical times, according to *Nelson's New Illustrated Bible Dictionary*:

> People were very conscious of the meaning of names. They believed that there was a connection between the name and the person it identified. A name somehow represented the nature of the person.
>
> This means that the naming of a baby was very important in the Bible. In choosing a name, the parents could reflect the circumstances of the child's birth, their own feelings, their gratitude to God, their hopes and prayers for the child, and their commitment of the child to God.[1]

What were their hearts feeling as they named him "Worship"?

_____

_____

His name became famous throughout Israel. Obed was the father of Jesse, the grandfather of David. Who was David?

_____

_____

Scholars believe the Book of Ruth was probably written after Israel realized David's importance as its greatest king. The family line closing this book starts back to Perez and ends at David. We know the rest of the history.

Who was born to this family line of Judah years later?

_____

It seems only fitting to end our lesson today with Mary, the mother of Jesus.

Mary was a young Jewish girl. She could have been as young as twelve or thirteen years old. She had recently become engaged to a carpenter named Joseph.

Mary honored God by keeping the Law of Moses. She also knew of the Old Testament prophesies about the coming Messiah. But she wouldn't have expected that God would choose her to be His mother. Think about it. Out of all the Jewish women of her time, God chose Mary!

When God sent Gabriel to announce to her His plan, she responded to God with belief and obedience. Even though she couldn't comprehend how she would conceive the Messiah, she trusted and accepted His plan.

Mary loved God. She was all in! She wasn't just in when it was convenient for her. He was her priority. She was all in, 100 percent!

Many women do noble things, but you surpass them all. (Proverbs 31:29)

Wrap Up: Our virtuous woman is all in as a disciple of the Lord. She knows His plan for her is beyond her comprehension, but she believes that He has the power and ability to bring it about. Her example to those watching is a commitment to total obedience to His teachings. Her legacy will impact generations to come.

Recently, I saw a TV interview of a young rising NBA star. The interviewer asked him the usual questions about certain plays of the game that had just ended. But it was the last question that I paid particular attention to. It went something like this: "How do you prepare yourself to play?" The player's reply went something like this: "I prepare myself by being ready when the coach calls my name!"

Are you listening for the Coach to call your name? Are you ready? Just like Mary, will you be all in?

Journal your response to the One who calls your name.

Endnotes:
[1]*Nelson's New Illustrated Bible Dictionary*, ed. Ronald F. Young-blood (Nashville: Thomas Nelson, 1995).

Royal Reflection

Today has been one of those days when every person that I have come in contact with has caused me to do a self-character examination. Sometime late in the afternoon, after being encouraged by the Lord to participate in this all-day event, two passages of Scripture came to my mind. The first is found in 1 Corinthians. The apostle Paul warned the church about disobedience using the example of when the Israelites were in the wilderness:

> These things happened to them as examples and were written down as warnings for us, on whom the fulfillment of the ages to come. *So, if you think you are standing firm, be careful that you don't fall!* No temptation has seized you except what is common to man. (1 Corinthians 10:11–13, emphasis added)

These verses confirm one reason that we shouldn't think too highly of ourselves. I don't know about you, but the Lord is faithful in bringing me back to reality when I do. The reality is the temptations that seize others are common to me also. When I judge someone for something they did or didn't do, I soon find myself doing the same thing! I am not referring to condoning the sins of others. I am referring to a critical spirit within ourselves where we try to mold others into our own image, when we ourselves are also falling short of perfection every day.

The other passage of Scripture that the Lord brought to my mind is located in 1 Peter.

[Your beauty] should be that of your inner self,
the unfading beauty of a gentle and quiet spirit,
which is great worth in God's sight. (1 Peter 3:4)

Peter says the beauty that does not fade is a humble and quiet spirit. Listen to what the Greek word means here for quiet. It indicates a tranquility arising from within, causing no disturbance to others.[1] When we judge the actions of another, believe me, disturbance comes to them!

This gentle and quiet spirit is not a personality trait! It is evidence of surrender to the Lord's teachings. As a daughter of the King, our daily walk is a testimony to how much or how little we are surrendered to His leadership. Our attitudes and actions as daughters should be a reflection of our Father, the King. Our position is of utmost importance to His kingdom. Don't shrink back; move forward with the Lord. Wear the crown of princess-status that's worthy of your calling.

Endnotes:
[1] James Strong, *The New Strong's Expanded Exhaustive Concordance of the Bible* (Nashville: Thomas Nelson, 2010).

She Fears the Lord

PROVERBS 31:30

Your age will likely determine how you respond to this introduction. If you are under forty, you may not get the next few sentences, but here goes: This morning, as I was getting ready for work, my 53-year-old self was looking back at me in the mirror. I said, "What happened?"

I can't believe I am the age I am! I mean, good grief, I'm getting mail from the Social Security Administration and AARP! Believe me, I realize that a lot of life has happened. But looking back, I feel that I only blinked a few times and time sped up. So here I am with less energy; graying, thinner hair; extra pounds; and the knowledge of what's to come—more aging.

KJV	NASB	NIV
Favour is deceitful, and beauty is vain; but a woman that feareth the LORD, she shall be praised.	Charm is deceitful and beauty is vain, but a woman who fears the LORD she shall be praised.	Charm is deceptive, and beauty is fleeting; but a woman who fears the LORD is to be praised.

Have you ever known a charmer? I have! He was tall, dark, and handsome, and he could charm his way in and charm his way out of anything. I saw him in action every day. If you have ever known or know a charmer, then you understand why Scripture says that charm is deceptive. Charmers learn quickly how far they can go and what they can get. It becomes, if not kept in check, a game deceiving those they are playing. If you have been told that you are a charmer, please be careful because "charm is deceptive, and beauty is fleeting."

I have never thought of myself as anything other than average looking. Oh, there's times that I say to Oatman, "I think I look cute in this outfit!" Of course, he always agrees. (He may be afraid not to!) Let's face it, sweet sister, as women we desire to be beautiful (or really cute)!

When was the last time you felt beautiful? Be honest. It's just us girls talking.

I told you in a previous lesson how much I love clothes. Well, I have to say, that is one way that I feel beautiful. There's nothing like a new outfit to get the senses flowing. I also love to go to the salon for a haircut and color.

What makes you feel beautiful?

_____

_____

Write 1 Peter 3:3–4.

If part of this is familiar to you, that's because it was in our last Royal Reflection. It is certainly worth repeating!

What is great worth to God?

A few years ago, our grandson, Jude, was spending a week with us. He was five years old at the time. One afternoon, while upstairs in my office, I heard little feet making their way up the stairs. Jude wanted to tell me everything he and his Papa had been doing outside. I listened and commented appropriately. Then he pulled up a chair next to me and looked at the computer screen as I worked.

He soon grew bored and his eyes fixed on me. I continued to work, but I could see him out of the corner of my eye checking me out. Then it happened! Yes, the unthinkable came out of that sweet precious mouth.

"Neener, you have the biggest ears I have ever seen!" It did give me some comfort that he was only five. I mean, really, he hadn't been on planet Earth that long! How many sets of ears could he have possibly seen?

Then, as his little head turned and looked at my ears from different views, he followed up with, "How did you ever grow them that big?"

I responded with, "I don't know."

You, my dear sibling, may be a drop-dead gorgeous woman, yet beauty is fleeting; but a woman who fears the Lord is to be praised.

I have studied the fear of the Lord and taught my Sunday school class for the last three weeks on this subject. To be honest, I'm still not settled in my heart that I have even come close to what it really means.

Nelson's Illustrated Bible Dictionary defines it this way: To fear the Lord is "a feeling of reverence, awe and respect."[1]

I have been in lots of different worship services and seen many ways people show reverence, awe, and respect for the Lord. And I have also witnessed the same at home, work, and even at the mall.

What are some ways you have seen this?

_____

_____

Regarding the fear of the Lord, what does it mean to you to have "awe" for the Lord?

_____

_____

Oatman is hunting this morning. He texted me a picture a few minutes ago of the sun coming up and said, "What a sunrise!

God is something!" Nothing profound, I know, but I know my husband. I guarantee, his eyes were fixed on that sunrise, but his heart had wrapped itself around its Artist. Not even the deer could have distracted him from his Creator. The "awe" that we feel over who He is and what He does is fear of the Lord.

What does it mean to you to have "reverence" for the Lord?

_____

_____

Every Monday morning, our church staff congregates at the altar for prayer. We are there to specifically pray for our church family and for each other. When we meet in the hallway to walk up to the sanctuary together, there is always talking and laughing taking place. But as we walk through the doors to the sanctuary, I have noticed that there's a stillness that comes over us as we take our place at the altar. For me there is such an awareness of God's presence. I realize that He was also downstairs in the hallway, but at that altar, I see Him as King, high and lifted up. I am His beloved servant, bowed at His feet with hurts, worries, defeats, feeling so unworthy of His presence. Yet there I am. Although He is King, His eyes are on me and the others gathered there. It is humbling and powerful. There's a reverence there that I can't explain. God is just being God, and we have no other choice than to respond with reverence toward Him.

What does it mean to you to have "respect" for the Lord?

_____

_____

Webster's Dictionary says that respect is "to feel or show honor or esteem for someone."[2]

It is not difficult to see how disrespectful the world has become. I saw a young man the other day walking behind an elderly woman entering a store. She was struggling to open the door. The man was right there watching her but never offered to help her. I also witness children speaking harshly and disrespectfully to their parents on a regular basis. Recently, our local news announced that a man had been arrested and charged with the murders of his father, mother, and sister. These are only a few examples of what we see and hear around us every day. When we are not honoring others, we are not honoring God.

We show Him high respect and reflect His character by living lives devoted to Him. It is not enough to merely honor Him outwardly. God desires honor from within our hearts.

Taking into account the examples I have given you and what God has revealed to you in your own mind, how would you personally define the fear of the Lord?

_____

_____

How do others see the fear of the Lord in you?

_____

_____

Fearing the Lord is a lifestyle for a Proverbs 31 woman. She depends on all that He is to her and in her. She knows that she is nothing without Him, but with Him she can do all things. She knows that He is who He says He is and that He loves her and will do what He says He will do. So, she trusts Him at His word, through His Word, and is simply obedient.

> **Charm is deceptive, and beauty is fleeting; but a woman who fears the LORD is to be praised. (Proverbs 31:30)**

Wrap Up: Our woman of noble character knows that true beauty is from within. Having the fear of the Lord makes her a breath-taking sight to see, and she is praised!

Journal your prayer.

Endnotes:
[1]*Nelson's New Illustrated Bible Dictionary*, ed. Ronald F. Young-blood (Nashville: Thomas Nelson,1995).
[2]*Webster's New World Dictionary*, Concise Ed., s.v. "respect."

She Is to be Praised

PROVERBS 31:31

According to *The Bible Knowledge Commentary*:

> The virtues of a noble wife are those that are
> extolled throughout the book of Proverbs: hard
> work, wise investments, good use of time, plan-
> ning ahead, care for others, respect for one's
> spouse, ability to share godly values with oth-
> ers, wise counsel, and godly fear (worship, trust,
> service, obedience). As Proverbs has stated
> repeatedly, these are qualities that lead to honor,
> praise, success, personal dignity, and worth, and
> enjoyment of life. In the face of the adulteress'_
> temptations mentioned often in Proverbs, it is
> fitting that the book concludes by extolling a
> virtuous wife. Young men and others can learn
> from this noble woman. By fearing God, they can
> live wisely and righteously. That is the message
> of Proverbs.[1]

KJV	NASB	NIV
Give her of the fruit of her hands; and let her own works praise her in the gates.	Give her the product of her hands, and let her works bring her praise at the gates.	Give her the reward she has earned, and let her works bring her praise at the city gate.

Our woman of noble character stood firm in her faith and did the work. She stayed true to herself by staying true to her God. The sanctifying work of the Spirit had created something so rare and beautiful within her. We have seen her through this journey persevere through challenges, difficulties, and blessings, keeping her head up, her hands working, and her heart in rhythm with the Father's.

Read James 2:14–26 in your Bible.

Focus in on verse 17: "In the same way, faith by itself, if it is not accompanied by action, is dead."

And verse 18: "Show me your faith without deeds, and I will show you my faith by what I do."

Do you see how faith (believing) and the actions we take because of our faith, go hand in hand?

Think about "the fruit of her hands" (KJV). She was driven by her faith and her love for God. What do you think the first part of this verse means? "Give her the reward (fruit of her hands)".

_____

_____

The Keil and Delitzsch Commentary on the Old Testament states: "The fruit of her hands is the good which, by her conduct, she has brought to maturity—the blessing which she has secured for others, but, according to the promise (Isaiah 3:10), has also secured for her own enjoyment. "[2]

Write "the promise" in Isaiah 3:10.

_____

_____

As we love God and invest in the lives of others out of our faith, we will enjoy our life. But, if you see our Proverbs 31 woman as a doer (deeds) and miss that above all she is a worshiper (faith) and try to mimic her, you will be worn out and discouraged. She is a worshiper because she fears the Lord. The deeds that follow are the result of that.

At the beginning of this study I told you that King Lemuel was most likely Solomon; therefore, Bathsheba would be the queen mother writing this to her son. No one knows for sure, but I don't think our study would be complete if we didn't focus a bit on Bathsheba.

This is a statement from Wikipedia concerning Bathsheba: "She is most known for the Bible story in which King David took her to sleep with him."[3] Everything within me cries out, "NO! Don't remember that about her!" Poor Bathsheba! If that is how she is remembered most, then I daresay we need to speak out for her. I will step forward and show you in Scripture that she was so much more than a night with the king!

Let's look at six different passages in which Bathsheba's name appears. I encourage you to read through the entirety of the sections that I will be referencing. I never want to take anything out of context by quoting a verse or two here and there. My intent is to only direct you to consider or reconsider the character of Bathsheba.

God has shown me through this study that Bathsheba was of great value to Him. She shows us strength, honor, endurance, confidence, and love. A woman who feared the God of Abraham, Isaac, and Jacob, the God she worshipped and obeyed.

2 Samuel 11:1–5:

King David was on his rooftop and saw beautiful Bathsheba bathing. "The reference to Bathsheba's bathing refers to a ritual of cleansing after completion of the seven days of impurity following her menstrual cycle. (Leviticus 15:19–24) It also establishes that she was within the most likely time for conception when she had sexual intercourse with David (10–14 days after commencement of menstruation)."[4]

This may be new to you, but Bathsheba was in the *mikveh*, a ritual bath designed for the Jewish rite of purification. "Jewish law prescribed that women immerse themselves in the waters of the *mikveh* following their menstrual periods ... in order to become ritually pure and permitted to resume sexual activity."[5]

Do you know what this means? She was not taking a bubble bath out where she knew the king would see her. She wasn't strategically trying to entice the king. She was following the law for the Jewish rite of purification because she feared the Lord.

Scripture states that David had Bathsheba brought to him. Bathsheba's reaction is not recorded. We shouldn't assume that she was a willing participant. To deny the king could have been her death sentence.

2 Samuel 11:6–27:

After Bathsheba's husband, Uriah, was killed, Bathsheba mourned. The Hebrew word, *caphad* for mourned, means "to tear the hair and beat the breasts; it means to wail."[6] Bathsheba obviously loved her husband and was devastated by his death. She mourned to the level of "tearing the hair and beating the breasts."

2 Samuel 12:1–23:

David and Bathsheba's baby was born but was very sick. Scripture records David fasting and praying for the child. But on the seventh day, the child died. Again, we see great loss for Bathsheba and she grieved. Scripture tells us that David comforted Bathsheba.

The Hebrew meaning for the word, comforted in 2 Samuel 12:24, means "with strength with repentance." When David came to Bathsheba, he came with godly sorrow for all that he had put her through. His grievous heart first confessed his sin to God. Psalm 51 is the prayer that he prayed to God after the prophet Nathan came to rebuke what he had done. In Scripture, David is the only one who was rebuked.

2 Samuel 12:24-25:

Bathsheba gave birth to a son and they named him Solomon. Because the Lord loved him, He told Nathan to name him Jedidiah, which means "Beloved by Yahweh." What joy Bathsheba must have felt to hold this baby, her son, especially after the loss of the first child with David. I don't know about you, but I want to know when little "Beloved by Yahweh" took his first steps, said his first words, and most of all, how he developed his heart for Almighty God. One thing I'm sure of is that his parents, King David and Bathsheba, taught him the ways of the Lord.

> Listen, my son, to your father's instruction and
> do not forsake your mother's teaching. They will
> be a garland to grace your head and a chain to
> adorn your neck. (Proverbs 1:8–9)

1 Kings 1:11–31:

At this time, King David was very old. Adonijah, David's son with Haggith, born next after Absalom, put himself forward as king. After hearing this through the prophet Nathan, Bathsheba went in to David's room and told him the plan of Adonijah. Nathan came in behind her to confirm what she had said as truth. The king said to Bathsheba,

> As surely as the LORD lives, who has delivered
> me out of every trouble, I will surely carry out
> today what I swore to you by the LORD, the God
> of Israel: Solomon your son shall be king after
> me, and he will sit on my throne in my place. (1
> Kings 1:29–30)

Bathsheba showed great courage and respect as she entered the room of the king. But there's something that I can't get away from: It's the respect David gave Bathsheba. I encourage you to read the entire chapter and see for yourself. Why would he show her such honor? Well, "give her the reward she has earned" comes to mind.

1 Kings 2:13–22:

After Solomon became king, Adonijah went to Bathsheba with a request that she speak to the king for him. He wanted

David's nurse, Abishag, to become his wife. I have thought about this segment of Scripture for days. I had questions that I needed answered. I had dug my heels into commentaries but was not successful in getting all the answers. I did, however, gain a better understanding of why this was a wrong thing to ask for. Let's talk about that first. All of David's possessions would have gone to the new king. This would have included David's nurse. As we read this passage, we might think, "What's the big deal?" It was a big deal. Adonijah was asking for something that belonged to the king. King Solomon had him put to death because of his request. To help us comprehend this, we have to go back to 1 Kings 1:49–52. Take a few minutes to read that now. The king had no choice because evil was found in him.

Now, let's get back to Bathsheba. Why did Adonijah come to Bathsheba in the first place? Well, I don't for a second believe she was a pushover. She was the queen mother and spoke as such (verses 13–14). Let me ask you this: Who do you go to when you want to make a case with someone that you can't, or feel you can't, personally approach? Of course, the one they are closest to—the one they will listen to. Here's my point—Adonijah chose Bathsheba because of the relationship she had with her son.

> When Bathsheba went to King Solomon to speak
> to him for Adonijah, the king stood up to meet
> her, bowed down to her and sat down on his
> throne. He had a throne brought for the king's
> mother, and she sat down at his right hand. "I
> have one small request to make of you," she said.
> "Do not refuse me." The king replied, "Make
> it, my mother; I will not refuse you." (1 Kings
> 2:19–20)

King Solomon stood up and bowed down to her. You may be thinking, "Yes, because she was the queen." But he didn't address her as queen, he addressed her as mother. When she walked into the throne room, he saw his mother. His actions were from the respect and honor he felt for her.

One last thing, Bathsheba's name means "daughter of the oath." We spent time studying vows at the beginning of this Bible study. Remember, King Lemuel was the son of the queen's vows? Look at the definitions below:

Vow – a solemn promise or pledge that binds a person to perform a specified act or to behave in a certain manner.[7]

Oath – a solemn statement or claim used to validate a promise.[8]

As we have already studied, Bathsheba, (if she was in fact the queen mother), had made promises to God concerning her son. I have great empathy for her as I consider all the loss she experienced. I hope that through this lesson you can better understand, as we examined the woman behind the name, why she made promises to God concerning her son. The time she spent with God talking to him about her son would explain the courage, confidence, and strength she exhibited as she moved to secure what God had given to him: the throne.

Ruth has been our shining example of the Proverbs 31 woman, but let's also give credit to the one who penned the character of this virtuous woman, the queen herself. As she considered all the attributes that springs out of any woman who puts God first, loving Him and serving Him above all things and people, these verses came forward. Our precious Ruth showed us how these attributes were lived out.

You see, sister, Bathsheba was the "daughter of the oath," the promise of God's eternal plan and purpose for those who accept His grace. Out of that acceptance, our lives are lived out in obedience to His teachings. I pray that you can celebrate with me today that through the life, death, and resurrection of Jesus, we have freedom from the curse of death, that all promises are "yes" in Him, and we have a glorious future that awaits us!

Give her the reward she has earned, and let her works bring her praise at the city gate. (Proverbs 31:31)

Wrap Up: Our woman of noble character earns praise and honor from the life she lives. By prioritizing God, she is empowered by His Spirit to accomplish what He would have her do according to His plan for her. She stands out to others, and they give her praise.

Record any insights into the character of Bathsheba that the Lord might have brought to your mind.

Close in prayer.

Endnotes:
[1]*The Bible Knowledge Commentary*, eds. John S. Walvoord and Roy B. Zuck (Colorado Springs: David C. Cook, 1983) .
[2]C. F. Keil and F. Delitzsch, *Keil and Delitzsch Commentary on the Old Testament*, New Updated Edition (Peabody, MA: Hendrickson Publishers, 1996).
[3]"Bathsheba," Wikipedia, https://en.wikipedia.org/wiki/Bathsheba.
[4]John H. Walton, Victor H. Matthews, and Mark W. Chavalas, *The IVP Bible Background Commentary: Old Testament* (Downers Grove, IL: InterVarsity Press, 2000).
[5]Beth Wenger, "Mikveh," Jewish Women's Archive, http://jwa.org/encyclopedia/article/mikveh.
[6]James Strong, *The New Strong's Expanded Exhaustive ConCordance of The Bible, Red-Letter Edition*, Dictionaries include contributions by John R. Kohlenberger(Nashville, TN: Thomas Nelson Publishers, 2001)
[7]*Nelson's New Illustrated Bible Dictionary*, ed. Ronald F. Youngblood (Nashville: Thomas Nelson,1995)
[8]Ibid.

Daughter, Where's Your Crown?

We have experienced the love of a queen mother toward her son. This mother desperately wanted her son, made in the image of God, to live as such. She had made promises to God concerning her son and she wasn't lax in fulfilling her responsibility in keeping those promises. With steadfastness, she led him in the ways of the Lord. Then her love moved her toward his future as she carefully listed the attributes of a woman she desired for him to choose. Not just any woman, but a woman of virtue like Ruth—a wise, loving, hardworking, compassionate, caring, generous woman who would always persevere to do the right thing out of her relationship with the Lord.

Just like most mothers, the queen wanted more for her son. Did she think he was settling for less than what he could have? Her advice certainly led to a higher way of living. Being king with all its authority, status, wealth, reputation and power would have been enough for most queens. But not for the one who knew the Source of peace, strength, contentment, and joy. She knew the "more" could only be found in a personal relationship with God.

We have also, through the pages of Scripture, traveled many miles with Ruth from Moab to Bethlehem. We have stayed on her heels and looked into her heart to see the woman of noble character. Ruth, though a foreigner, accepted God's great love for her and devoted her life to loving Him back by serving Him.

I don't know what your journey with Him has been like over the last few weeks. But I know Him well enough to know that His Word has taught, convicted, and maybe even brought healing to you. His Word is power and will do the work it sets out to do.

Life can be hard. Life can be sad. Life can be devastating. Life doesn't always turn out like we want it to. But here's what I have learned as I continue to walk through this life with my Savior.

- I will not know Him as Comforter if I don't have times of sadness and uncertainty when His comfort holds me close.
- I will not know Him as Counselor if I don't allow Him to counsel me as I make everyday life choices.
- I will not know Him as Deliverer if I don't see His deliverance over me as He stands on every promise He has ever made.
- I will not know Him as Almighty God if I am unaware of how He protects me.
- I will not truly know Him as the God of love if I never experience His grace and mercy for myself.
- And I will not know Him as the King of Kings and Lord of Lords if I fail to exalt Him and praise Him as God of all in all circumstances.

You may be in a season of struggle right now. If you entered into this study with sadness, confusion, anger and/or exhaustion, you are in good company. As I think back over the last two and a half years since I began studying and writing, I am amazed and even appalled at life's stuff that I have endured. That's why I feel at liberty to talk to you frankly about what has been confirmed to me over and over again.

As women—daughters, sisters, wives, mothers, friends—we desire more for ourselves and those we love. God has instructed me to tell you that this world's "more" is not lasting and will not satisfy long-term. Jesus is the "more" you hunger for, the "more" you are searching for. Immerse yourself into the one relationship that will make you whole! It sounds simple, and it is, but not without a great deal of challenges. You will be challenged, I promise, every day. But stay the course, and you will see the fruit that God will produce in you!

The Lord led me to Psalm 8 after giving me the name of this study a few years ago when He first placed the desire in my heart to write it. I made a note in my Bible, but to be honest, never thought any more about it until He reminded me a few days ago.

Let's take a look:

> O LORD, our Lord, how majestic is your name in
> all the earth!
> You have set your glory above the heavens.
> From the lips of children and infants you have
> ordained praise because of your enemies, to
> silence the foe and the avenger.
> When I consider your heavens, the work of your
> fingers, the moon and the stars, which you have
> set in place, what is man that you are mindful of
> him, the son of man that you care for him?
> You made him a little lower than the heavenly
> beings and crowned him with glory and honor.
> You made him ruler over the works of your
> hands, you put everything under his feet: all

flocks and herds, and the beasts of the field, the
birds of the air, and fish of the sea, all that swim
the paths of the seas.
O LORD, our Lord, how majestic is your name in
all the earth! (vv. 1–9)

He has crowned us with glory and honor! That word crowned
in the Hebrew means "encircled": for attack or protection according to *Strong's Expanded Exhaustive Concordance of the Bible*.

The Lord is not only mindful of us, but in all His wisdom, He
has entrusted us to continue until our work here is complete.
Yet, He hasn't left us alone. He has filled us with His Spirit and
encircled us with His presence and status so that we are able to
fight the battle against the enemy and live lives we are worthy
of as His daughters. You are His beloved princess. Your crown is
secure. "You did not receive a spirit that makes you a slave again
to fear again, but you received the Spirit of [daughtership]" (Romans 8:15).

We belong to Jesus, so our story is a "happily ever after" story. Each chapter of our life will look different as we live it out,
but because God is God, we can always look forward to the next
chapter.

Princess, loved and empowered by God, go live your life with
your "more" and enjoy your "happily ever after."

With much love,

Kathy

About the Author

Kathy Farley lives on a farm near Murray, Kentucky, with her husband, Oatman. They share three grown children and three grandchildren. Oatman and Kathy enjoy their family, camping, and Murray State University basketball.

Kathy's love for the Word of God opened a door twenty-five years ago to a teaching ministry. She began teaching a group of women on Sunday mornings. A few years later she added a class where she wrote and taught her own curriculum on Sunday nights.

Kathy knew that God was calling her into full-time ministry. As she waited for His timing, He continued the process of preparing her through a Christian organization, Walk to Emmaus, by giving her speaking opportunities as well as ministry assignments behind the scenes of the weekend retreats.

The journey continued as God filled Kathy with the desire to write a devotional book, *God's Arms Are Big Enough—Rest in His Promises*, which was published in 2008. During this time, churches began calling her to speak at various women's events in the area.

In 2011, she stepped into a full-time ministry position on staff at her church as an administrative assistant. Once again, God placed a desire back in her heart to write, this time a Bible study. He remained faithful in giving her the words to write as she dug in her heels. You are holding in your hands that study, ***Daughter, Where's Your Crown? Examine Biblical Virtue in the Life of Ruth and Proverbs 31.***

Kathy loves the Lord with her whole heart. She has a desire for women of all ages to experience freedom in Christ from everything that is keeping them from a life of wholeness in Him. She looks forward to what God has next in this journey of life.